DAMON HILL

World Champion

DAMON HILL
World Champion

David Tremayne

Photographs by
John Townsend

Weidenfeld & Nicolson
LONDON

CONTENTS

1

MR MOTOR RACING

WHEN GRAHAM HILL CRASHED HIS PLANE
INTO A TREE ON ARKLEY GOLF COURSE NEAR
ELSTREE ON THE FOG-CHILLED NIGHT OF
29 NOVEMBER 1975, KILLING HIMSELF AND
FIVE MEMBERS OF HIS EMERGENT FORMULA ONE
TEAM, THE NATION MOURNED NOT ONLY THE
LOSS OF A GREAT BRITISH SPORTSMAN, BUT
THE MAN WHO HAD BECOME THE ULTIMATE
AMBASSADOR FOR MOTOR RACING.

That fateful Saturday was a foul evening, with a dripping fog wreathing the environs of Elstree where the countryside of Hertfordshire crept gently towards the suburbia of north London. Not far away were the Haberdashers Aske's School for Boys, where fifteen-year-old Damon Graham Devereux Hill was being educated, and the beautiful detached house which stood in its own grounds at Shenley, where the Hill family lived and Bette, Graham's wife, was entertaining guests. At the small airstrip nearby, several cars stood in the damp air, awaiting owners who would never return.

The Embassy Hill Racing team had been testing its new car at the Paul Ricard circuit in the south of France, welcoming the chance to escape the approach of British winter. More clement weather would allow it to put the first

meaningful miles on the new machine that team owner Graham Hill believed would propel his driver Tony Brise firmly into the top three of Grand Prix racing.

Earlier that year the veteran driver had finally taken the hardest decision of his life and retired from active racing. At the British GP at his beloved Silverstone in July he had driven an emotional lap of honour in one of his own cars, helmetless, saying goodbye to his thousands of fans. He drove with one hand and waved with the other, his mane of dark hair whipped by the wind. He was renowned for his stiff upper lip, upon which bristled that famous moustache, but that day the dampness in his eyes owed nothing to the passage of air blasted across them. Graham Hill knew that he was finally calling it a day after seventeen years in Formula One, passing on the torch after a competition career that few could aspire to rival.

The long goodbye. At Silverstone during the 1975 British Grand Prix, Graham Hill drove an emotional lap to bid farewell to his fans on the day he retired as a driver.

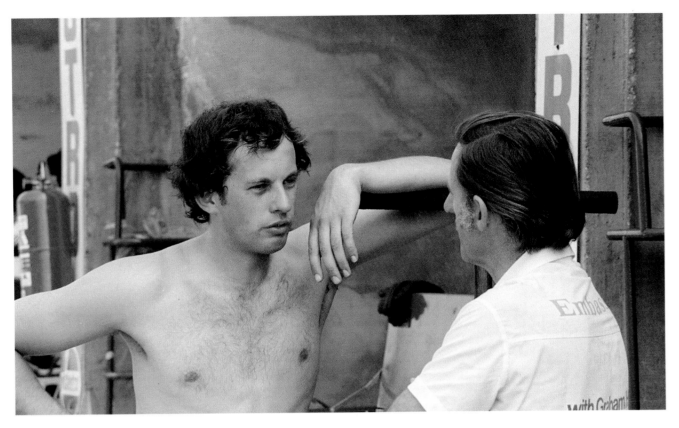

Tony Brise was brash and brilliant and his relationship with Graham Hill gelled immediately. The combination of champion and charger held so much promise for 1976...

His friends rejoiced, for though he had been less competitive in recent years, since a typically dogged comeback from a leg-breaking accident at Watkins Glen in late 1969, the risks had not changed. They had feared that, like record breaker Donald Campbell, he too would be tempted to prod the tiger once too often. Among them there was profound relief.

In Brise, however, a brash young karter who had leaped to prominence in one of Hill's cars during that very year, he knew that he had found a soulmate in whom he could place his faith, a brilliant star in the making whom he could tutor in the finer points, and whose outstanding natural talent promised to provide the other essential elements for success at the highest level. If the new GH2 works, said the pundits, watch out for Brise and Hill in 1976.

Hill was advised to land at Luton Airport, some thirty miles further north, but that would have entailed a coach or taxi ride back to Elstree, and he was trying to get his mechanics back in time for an official dinner in London. The Lotus chief, Colin Chapman, had once shown him a special flight path into Elstree, and he was confident that he could pull off the feat. In the fog, however, he lost his bearings and he and all of his passengers – Brise, designer Andy Smallman, team manager Ray Brimble, and mechanics Tony Alcock and Terry Richards – died instantly when the Piper Aztec plunged into a tree and cartwheeled.

At Shenley, white-faced Damon Hill ran into the kitchen where his mother was just answering a call from a newspaper reporter who had asked her bluntly: 'Is it true about Graham Hill?' In his book *Graham*, Neil Ewart records that she remembered she had just started to think, 'Oh, crikey – now what?' when Damon blurted out: 'Mummy, a plane has crashed in fog at Arkley golf course on its way from Marseilles to Elstree . . . They think it's Daddy.'

With the usual decorum of the British media, names had not been disclosed in the television report that Damon and his sister Samantha had just watched, but they knew instinctively that their father had been involved. A legend of motor racing had just perished in the fog.

Graham Hill was more than just a double World Champion, and the only man ever to

THROUGH THEIR MUTUAL LOVE OF MOTORCYCLES THEY STARTED TO FORM THE SORT OF FATHER-SON BONDING THAT THE RACING DRIVER'S HECTIC TRAVEL SCHEDULE HAD COMPROMISED.

Champion year. Graham Hill won the title for the first time in 1962 for BRM, after a season-long battle with Jim Clark and Lotus.

win that elusive Triple Crown: the World Championship, the Indianapolis 500 and the Le Mans 24 Hours. He was a national institution. At the time of his death his only son was an introspective youth who was only beginning to perceive and, perhaps, understand the unusual motivations that drove his father. Through their mutual love of motorcycles they were just starting to form the sort of father-son bonding that the racing driver's hectic travel schedule had hitherto compromised.

Damon was sent off to the Californian homes of American World Champion Phil Hill, who was no relation but an understanding friend, and former BRM team-mate Dan Gurney. There, in a daze, he gradually began to piece his own life together and to come to terms with his loss. Back in England, his mother Bette and sisters Samantha and Brigitte also slowly began to adjust to the unpalatable facts of the life that lay ahead for them. There were irregularities in Hill's paperwork related to the requirements of the Civil Aviation Authorities, and insurance claims from the families of the other team members that cost Bette Hill almost everything. Her family didn't quite go from riches to rags, but its circumstances were dramatically re-

duced. In one week this brave woman went to six funerals, one her husband's, whom she had worshipped, the others his friends whose families were now, some reluctantly, obliged to make legal claims against his estate. Stronger personalities would have been crushed by the ignominy of it all, as financial problems were piled so swiftly upon tragic personal loss. Instead, Bette and her children fought back.

Norman Graham Hill: his personality, his ghost even, flits throughout the ensuing story. To enthusiasts in their hundred thousands the world over, he was Mr Motor Racing. He was the perfect ambassador for British motorsport, with his erect bearing, clipped speech and slim military moustache. Today we are used to Nigel Mansell's popularity with mass audiences, but Hill was every bit as lauded, the affection more genuine, for this was not yet the age of brutal xenophobia in sport where anyone capable of beating foreign competition is automatically

By 1968 Clark was dead, and Hill led the shattered Lotus team to his second championship after fighting all the way with Clark's natural successor, Jackie Stewart

adopted by some elements with little or no knowledge of his actual discipline. The masses knew Graham Hill not just from his racing but from his numerous television appearances, which had suggested that an alternative career as a comedian awaited him whenever he hung up his helmet. Throughout the sport there was tremendous admiration for him. He loved his motor racing wholeheartedly, and even the man in the street recognised just how much he had put back into the sport.

He had made it to the top on his own efforts. In his early days nobody gave him anything. It all came through sheer persistence, hard work and blatant opportunism. As Damon later would, he began his career on motorbikes, taking part in scrambles and rallies, and his path to success is strewn with examples of that ability to turn nothing into something. He talked his way into another driving school job on the strength of his four-lap experience at the first. He signed on the dole and travelled to Westerham in Kent from north London every day while his father thought he was off at a 'proper' job. He haunted the then-popular Steering Wheel Club so frequently that nobody ever thought to question whether he had actually paid a membership fee.

He was second in his first heat and fourth in the final of his first race, at Brands Hatch in a Cooper 500 in April 1954, and after that he never looked back. Tirelessly he exploited his services as a mechanic to get himself regular drives in other people's cars.

That first year he met Colin Chapman at Brands Hatch at the August Bank Holiday event and became an unshakeable attachment to the emergent Team Lotus. He was beached, completely out of money, unable even to afford the fare back to London. Without a second thought he hitched a ride back in the team van, and Chapman immediately assumed he was a friend of partner Mike Costin's, just as Mike

NINETEEN YEARS AFTER HIS FATHER AND THE SMALL TEAM HE HAD BUILT DIED ON ARKLEY GOLF COURSE, DAMON HILL TOOK THE SAME OXFORD BLUE HELMET INTO BATTLE AGAIN.

was assuming he must be a friend of Colin's. Neither discovered their mistake straight away, and by the time he arrived back home Hill had talked himself into a mechanic's role with the team.

It was a long while before the awkward teenager Damon was finally able to express his feelings and his grief, and longer still before he began to feel the same competitive stirrings that had set his father on course for the race track. But once the stirrings had developed into an obsession, their careers would follow an eerily similar path.

Now, nineteen years after his father and the small team he had built died on Arkley golf course, Damon Hill takes the same Oxford blue helmet into battle again at the head of an F1 field. Graham had been a keen oarsman – 'Because I like sports where I can sit down!' – and the helmet's famous eight vertical white flashes represent the oar blades of the London Rowing Club. It seemed only natural that his son should wear the same distinctive helmet. Being the scion of a famous family can be a double-edged sword, as Gina Campbell in particular has found out. The English have always been uptight about nepotism, real or imagined. The Americans take a more relaxed view. Sons attempting to emulate deeds of famous fathers are actively encouraged, rather than discouraged, as Al Unser Jnr and Michael Andretti would testify. In Europe you have to go back to Alberto Ascari before you find a son whose own performances earned him what some perceive as the right to be compared with an illustrious parent. It's as if some devoted observers are offended by unsuccessful attempts by sons to live up to their fathers' great reputations.

Graham Hill was approaching forty when his team-mate at Lotus, Jim Clark, was killed, and this was a time when motor racing was spawning fresh young championship contenders such as Jackie Stewart and Jochen Rindt. As Denny Hulme would do two years later, after Bruce

McLaren's death, Hill quelled his own emotions in the aftermath of Hockenheim, and somehow found the reserves to lead Lotus back. He won the Spanish GP at Jarama, and went on to take his second title.

In chillingly similar circumstances, Damon Hill would lead the shattered Williams team back after Ayrton Senna's tragic death at Imola in 1994, winning the Spanish GP at Barcelona.

It was said of Graham Hill that he lacked Clark's natural flair, that he really had to work at everything he did. The same has been said of Mansell in comparison with Senna. Yet both Hill and Mansell enjoyed sterling successes. Now, by happy irony, one of racing's wheels has come full circle. If Hill had much in common with Mansell, and Mansell was the last man successfully to turn test driving duties into a regular drive with the same team, it is wholly apposite that the man who replaced him at Williams should be Damon, another to have achieved that trick.

He, too, would don the mantle of Grand Prix victor in time, and then he, too, would suffer the same damning comparisons with Senna and Michael Schumacher, being tagged the 'worker' compared to the great 'naturals'.

The waves of father's and son's stories lap against a familiar shore on many occasions, but it says everything about Damon Hill that when he finally broke into Grand Prix racing he did so on his own terms, and on his own merits, not because he was The Son of Graham Hill.

When Damon Hill went racing he did it on his own terms, but the Oxford blue helmet and its eight vertical white stripes were a legacy of his father.

Graham Hill is lost in thought at Monza in 1967, where a bored seven-year-old Damon ignores sisters Samantha and Brigitte. Racing had yet to captivate him.

2
HUMBLE BEGINNINGS

ANXIOUS TO MAKE HIS OWN MARK, DAMON
HILL FIRST SHOWED COMPETITIVE LEANINGS
TOWARDS MOTORCYCLES, AND HE WOULD
RETURN TO THEM FOR A WHILE AFTER
HIS FIRST FOUR-WHEEL OUTING PROVED
A LAMENTABLE FAILURE.

After Graham Hill's death his family had some desperate readjustments to make, financial and emotional. Damon still chooses his words carefully when he talks about it.

'It's wrong to say having a famous dad was difficult. Of course there were the advantages of fame and wealth – a trials bike, good education, nice holidays. But from the first moment at primary school you'd be singled out; people would smile at you and make references. I was six when Dad won Indy, eight when he took his second World Championship. I didn't give a jot then, but people around you respond. It could be embarrassing in front of friends, when you wanted to be the same as them. But it wasn't difficult. I didn't know anything different.

'The loss of my father was much worse than anything else. You can always replace things, but you can't reverse the death of your father.

'I didn't feel anything about what happened for years, although some of the aftermath made me very angry at times. Sometimes now I keep feeling it would be nice to have had a father around, so we could share things together. I didn't see much of Dad, but he had an enormous influence on me, on my attitude and sense of humour.'

Damon first became fascinated with the idea of racing motorbikes while his father was in the process of a somewhat fortuitous victory in the Daily Express International Trophy race at Silverstone in 1971, driving the distinctive lobster-claw Brabham BT34 for the team which had then just passed into the hands of Bernie Ecclestone, now the tsar of Formula One. Damon watched someone riding around the paddock on a 50cc monkey bike, and it was not long before he used his nascent powers of persuasion to have a go himself. He used them again after choosing a suitable moment of parental good humour, and admits that he was staggered when his father duly obliged his request by buying him a similar bike when he had passed his eleven-plus exams. It was quickly followed by a 350cc Bultaco, which started off as Graham's but soon passed to him. He coped well with the greater power, moving Hill senior to describe him as a natural rider. By this time, as Damon freely admits, he was bored by cars. Like many children of famous parents, he had tended to take for granted what they did for a living, and perhaps subconsciously had looked around for his own means of making a mark, his own furrow to plough. Motorbikes had provided the perfect answer.

In 1976 the thought of actually racing them took a firmer hold when he went to watch the Trans-Atlantic Trophy races at Brands Hatch with Barry Sheene and Kenny Roberts. 'I was starting to get interested in motor racing in 1975, and wanted to understand what was going on, but I never got any indication of whether Dad might approve,' he said.

Damon was never afraid of

FOR BETTE HILL THEY CANNOT HAVE BEEN EASY TIMES, AS SHE WATCHED HER SON ASPIRING TO EMULATE HER LATE HUSBAND.

Looking back, that famous helmet now looks out of place on a motorcycle but this was how Hill began his career. Success on this Kawasaki at Brands Hatch won him his national racing licence.

Portrait of the racer as a young man. Nineteen-year-old Hill finished eighth on this Kawasaki in the Joe Francis Motors Trophy race at Brands Hatch.

hard work to get what he wanted, a product of his upbringing and also the rearrangement he had had to make in the aftermath of his father's death. Commuting from St Albans, where the family had moved after selling the big house in Shenley, he worked as a building labourer to finance his aspirations, and then started bike racing – at Brands, naturally – in 1981 with a Kawasaki. Later he would work as a motorcycle messenger, but the long hours necessary to raise the money, and then to prepare the machinery, frequently took their toll in the form of minor accidents in the races in which he took part.

For Bette Hill these cannot have been easy times, as she watched her son aspiring to emulate her late husband. If there wasn't the pain of memory, there was the worry of injury, especially after the numerous falls. But Bette Hill was always made of stern stuff, and gave her son her wholehearted support.

Right up until he reached the heights of Formula One, where respect for the families of past heroes is negligible and passes are like gold dust, she could usually be relied upon to surface somewhere in the pits, holding a stopwatch the way she had for so many years when it was her husband and not her son racing. Once, at a biting cold, wet Formula Three qualifying session in 1986, she remained at her post when Damon had pitted for good, steadfastly keeping the watch on his team-mate Paul Radisich even though her hands were blue and numb. It was what she used to do when Jackie Stewart and Jimmy Clark were Graham's team-mates in the sixties, and she would not be persuaded to stop until the second car motored slowly down the pit lane. 'I don't want Paul to think we're only interested in what happens to Damon,' she said. Such was the woman who even went to the extent of paying for a racing drivers' course for her son at the Winfield School at Magny-Cours.

John Webb was the colourful, occasionally prickly supremo who ran Brands Hatch on behalf of Grovewood Securities. A frequently misunderstood man, he disguised a heart of gold behind a sometimes gruff exterior and often appeared to like nothing better than a public argument, especially in the evening hours. But he was also a man who remembered his friends, and Graham Hill had been one of them. Webb also had a nose for publicity which had more often than not put Brands Hatch in the headlines. When Hill decided that he might like to try racing on four

wheels, Webb put together a deal that helped them both.

'At the start of my bike-racing career I had patchy success,' said Damon, 'so at the end of 1983 I decided to try cars. John organised me an Argo JM16 for the BBC Grandstand series.'

One leading F3 team manager who witnessed his early races in this car, later told me: 'I felt sorry for the kid. He just didn't seem to have a clue what he was doing.'

Simon Arron, the editor of *Motor Sport* but at that time Club Racing Editor of its weekly racing sister *Motoring News*, recalled Hill's first competitive effort on four wheels.

'I remember being annoyed that the telex had rattled into life on a Tuesday afternoon, announcing that Damon Hill would be making his car racing début at Brands Hatch the following Sunday, 6 November. Annoyed, because it meant that the story arrived too late for that week's *MN*.

'The whole thing smacked a little bit of hype. Sons of famous racing drivers were an emerging breed, and Brands Hatch was very good at finding column inches in the national press in those days. A winter clubbie early in November would usually have no more than a dozen names on the press attendance list, if that, most of them local journalists. On this occasion, there were representatives of Fleet Street all over the place.

'I met Damon briefly in the paddock, on his way from the café to the team truck, and he said that he hoped he'd be able to raise the money to race full time the following year. He didn't sound terribly convinced about it all though, nor did he look as if he was enjoying himself greatly. Hardly surprising, because he'd only sat in the car for the first time a couple of days before the race. It wasn't ideal preparation, and the presence of Fleet Street didn't exactly help him to focus on his driving.

'Formula Ford 2000 was very competitive at the time, and in the circumstances it wasn't ex-

In 1987 the Hill GH2 was given an airing, and during a private test Damon did some brief laps. It was the first time it had run since the Paul Ricard tests in November 1975.

'SOME PEOPLE RESENTED THE FACT THAT HE'D BEEN GIVEN A DECENT DRIVE BECAUSE OF WHO HE WAS, BUT IN REALITY IT COULD HAVE DONE HIM MORE HARM THAN GOOD.'

actly a shock that he failed to qualify. He did get to race, however, because there was a multiple pile-up on about the second lap and there had to be a restart. With several cars sidelined, Damon was called up as first reserve.

'He trailed around at the back of the field, spinning a couple of times. He made a pit stop at one point. Apparently, he'd wanted to stop, but team manager John Kirkpatrick persuaded him to rejoin. The Brands Hatch PR machine might have had the best intentions, but headlines such as those in the following day's *Daily Mail*, which featured a picture spread entitled 'Demon Damon in a Spin', were hardly likely to enhance self-esteem or credibility.

'At the time I felt desperately sorry for him. Some people resented the fact that he'd been given a decent drive because of who he was, but in reality it could have done him more harm than good. It spoke volumes for his determination, and his potential, that he was able to jump into the cut-and-thrust world of junior Formula

Ford the following season and hold his own against the likes of Johnny Herbert and Mark Blundell.'

The Argo was run on behalf of Manadient Racing by Kirkpatrick, universally known within the sport as 'Kilt'. He now runs the Jim Russell Racing Drivers' School at Donington Park and has coached countless aspiring young men. Many of them have had the fear of God instilled in them after a tongue lashing from the feisty Scot. He remembers Damon's historic first outing all too well.

'He was bloody hopeless! And I'm sure by his own admission he would agree. What happened was that John Webb asked us to run him. I told him that I thought it was too soon, since Damon hadn't done anything. He wasn't ready. Webbie told me that Damon was too old and couldn't afford to waste time in 1600. He told me that either we could run him, or he'd find someone else. Well, the way the economy was at that time, it wasn't the sort of thing we could af-

Eleven years earlier Bette Hill had handed over the unique GH2 to the National Motor Museum at Beaulieu, where she is accompanied by daughter Brigitte and Lord Montagu. Damon looks pensive.

ford to turn down, so we did it! I remember that Webbie's cheque arrived the very next day!

'The publicity that race got was just ridiculous. I've got a book of press clippings on that one day alone. Damon's race was . . . ordinary. And the pictures in the newspapers were of him sitting parked across the road at the bottom of Paddock Bend. Really, he just didn't have any idea. He'd gone well there on bikes, and he was using biking lines. Well, we'd done a press day and a little bit of testing, but all he'd done before in cars was the Winfield course. It was all a bit bloody silly, to be honest. There were drivers out there like Anthony Reid and Julian Bailey, it was heavyweight stuff. Damon was a danger to himself and to everyone else.

'And yes, I seem to remember that he did ask if he could stop. I think it was after one of his spins, he came into the pits and said that he didn't think that he should carry on. Well, if

As ever, when support was needed Damon's then girlfriend Georgie and mother Bette, were on hand. On the Argo debut the press was also there in force.

you want to be a racing driver you race, so I think I sent him out again. I'm sure that's the way it happened.'

Those familiar with Kilt's lectures on driving etiquette know that you do not argue with his instructions. Hill returned to the race, but finished well down. 'There were three or four

races in the series, and he did nothing in them either,' says Kirkpatrick. 'Nothing at all.'

Hill makes no bones about the problems he encountered in those early days. 'Cars were a total culture shock,' he admits. 'All of a sudden I had to fiddle with the vehicle rather than simply trying harder to go faster. It was no longer a matter of getting good tyres and checking that the chain wasn't loose, and the cornering was so much faster.' He went back to bikes in early 1984, preferring once again to be the guy to beat rather than the butt of jokes. He competed in the Pro-Am Championship with a Yamaha LC350 and with a beloved TZ350 in the Champion of Brands series, taking more than forty wins.

Cars, however, were finally winning the battle for his affections. Later that year Kirkpatrick went along with him when he put a sponsorship proposal to Ricoh, the Japanese manufacturer of office equipment. The first glimmer of hope in what would become a successful motor-racing career became evident when the marketing department agreed to a deal. Damon Hill was finally ready to go motor racing properly.

'We had managed to persuade him to do Formula Ford 1600 with us,' says Kirkpatrick. 'Really, Webbie had been out of order expecting him to jump straight into Ford 2000. It was just too much for a beginner, having to think about wings and slick tyres and all that stuff when he needed just to be concentrating on racing. Late in 1984, once Damon had done the deal with Ricoh, Manadient ran a bog-standard Van Diemen for him, and he started to progress almost immediately. We had John Pratt in the team and he certainly helped Damon a lot. Really, it was almost like starting again. It was the first time that he'd had a sensible programme.'

He celebrated by scoring his maiden victory

In his first full season of motorsport, Hill raced wheel-to-wheel with the likes of the late Peter Rogers in the roughhouse world of Formula Ford.

at Brands Hatch in August, and that was sufficient to win him a Special Commendation in the end-of-season Grovewood Awards. I was a member of the judging panel, and was not the only one to be impressed by his improvement in a mere half season.

Initially our relationship got off to a wary start, following an incident earlier in the year when a national newspaper had published a comment he denies having made to illustrate the suggestion that he was a spoiled kid, and it was picked up in the letters page of *Motoring News*. He admitted good-naturedly that he detested our paper for a while, but really the whole thing was out of context. In the intervening years he never once came across as arrogant, bitter, jaded or spoiled, even in the darkest times. Indeed, he usually exudes an engaging charm that will undoubtedly stand him in good stead as his stature grows. He even became a columnist for us in 1993, when his F1 career took off.

1985 brought his first full season of racing, and showed the value of experience. This was the season in which several young drivers who would later emerge as his F1 rivals cut their teeth in the highly competitive world of

Formula Ford, using specially designed single-seater racing cars powered by almost standard Ford 1.6-litre engines. As Hill honed his talent, he did so wheel-to-wheel with Herbert, Blundell and the Belgian Bertrand Gachot. He earned a reputation for speed allied to boldness that occasionally bordered on the reckless, and it took him to six victories and third place in the prestigious Esso Championship. He was fifth in the Townsend Thoresen series, and when he finished third in the Formula Ford Festival at Brands Hatch – the category's most important event of the year – he had finally laid the ghost of that dreadful début two seasons earlier.

Shortly afterwards Jim Wright, who at the time worked for Eddie Jordan Racing but would shortly move across to run the sponsorship programme for mobile-phone company Cellnet's racing début, arranged a test session for him in an F3 car with EJR.

'I persuaded Eddie that we ought to give Damon a run, and eventually Eddie agreed, although Damon – or at least, Ricoh – had to pay for it! He was quick, too, lapping Donington very little slower than Mauricio Gugelmin, who had just won that year's championship.'

A fresh chapter had begun.

3

THE ROAD TO FORMULA ONE

MOTOR RACING IS NO RESPECTER OF FAMOUS NAMES.
DAMON HILL KNEW RIGHT FROM THE START THAT BEING
THE SON OF A DOUBLE WORLD CHAMPION WOULD IN
ITSELF BE NO PASSPORT TO FORMULA ONE. INSTEAD,
HAVING BORROWED £100,000, HE DETERMINED TO
MAKE HIS WAY TO THE TOP BY SQUEEZING THE
MAXIMUM FROM EACH AND EVERY OPPORTUNITY
THAT PRESENTED ITSELF.

Like his father, Damon Hill is made of determined mettle. Once he had suppressed his initial misgivings and decided that a career in motor racing was indeed what he really wanted, his persistence would slowly pay off as he began the arduous trek through the nursery slopes of the sport. At times it would be a soul-destroying process, but as each chance came along, so he made the most of it.

At the end of 1985 everything was going well, and Ricoh had agreed in principle to finance the vital graduation from Formula Ford to Formula Three. Where the former teaches the driver the rudiments of car control and racecraft, the latter is the category that most often hones a driver's talents for a future career in Formula 3000 and Formula One. The cars are smaller-scale versions of their Grand Prix brethren with the important distinction that they lack sheer horsepower. The onus is thus thrown on the driver not only to develop the smoothest possible style and to learn to preserve momentum and carry his speed through corners, but also to master the complex art of chassis set-up. This means understanding what goes into adjusting its suspension, as well as having a good working knowledge of its aerodynamics.

With the Japanese company's support, Hill would have a head start by racing alongside the established Formula Ford 2000 champion Bertrand Fabi at West Surrey Racing. This small but highly professional team was run by New Zealander Dick Bennetts, who had already masterminded F3 championships for Stefan Johansson, Jonathan Palmer, Ayrton Senna and Mauricio Gugelmin. It was widely acknowledged to be the best team in the business.

Any warm feelings Damon had, however, had evaporated before Christmas when Ricoh suddenly informed him that it would not be continuing after all. At a stroke, the foundation not only for his plans but his career too had been destroyed.

A tense period followed, for at all costs he had to rescue the situation before Bennetts was obliged to take another driver who had the right budget. The radiator company Warmastyle was interested for a while until it decided instead to sponsor the driver-assistance scheme called Racing for Britain. But there was still a chance of support when Hill topped its voting nominations, which were made by public members. At that time, however, he was managed by a company called Leisure 10/12, and the two parties could not agree terms.

Hill recalls those grim days. 'Ricoh pulled out just before Christmas and, without exaggeration, I didn't leave the phone or the office. I was there Christmas Day and Boxing Day, putting calls through to the most ridiculous people – some really obscure ones! – just to find something. *Anything*. I was absolutely desperate!

'Commercial deals don't just happen, and after the Warmastyle deal deflated came the problem with Racing for Britain. In retrospect that was the biggest mistake, turning down what was offered there.'

Desperate times called for desperate measures. He borrowed a large sum of money – said to be around £100,000 – from a source that was never identified, and dredged up on Dick Bennetts's doorstep once again. It has often been suggested that Damon's godfather, former team owner John Coombs, was the benefactor, but all parties have steadfastly maintained a dignified silence on the matter.

'The way I saw things I just had to be racing. I'd read one of Niki Lauda's books and I figured if I was really convinced I could do it I'd take a gamble and let things sort themselves out. I borrowed a huge sum on the understanding that it would be paid back. Money still has a fixed value as far as I am concerned. To get into F3 I did the deal with Dick which bought us the time to repay the loan.'

Tragedy was lurking, though, for Fabi was killed in an accident while testing at Goodwood early in 1986. Bennetts was devastated, and at the last minute changed his plans and switched to run Gugelmin in Formula 3000. Hill was left on the sidelines again.

'I could have said "Forget it" after Bert's death,' he confessed. 'Dick went through the same thing – everyone involved questioned the whole reason for racing. The darker side of the sport is thankfully rare, but I remember Dad

Andy Wallace and Maurizio Sandro Sala fought out the 1986 British F3 Championship. Here at Snetterton that year a rapidly developing Hill put them under pressure.

Entrant Glenn Waters puts the final touches to Hill's Ralt prior to the most important F3 race of his career, at Zandvoort in 1987. It brought him his first big win.

coming home one day very, very quiet and saw the news film of Jim Clark's death, but I wasn't too sure what it all meant. I was only eight.

'When Bert was killed I took the conscious decision that I wasn't going to stop doing that sort of thing. It's not just competing, it's doing something exciting. I'm at my fullest skiing, racing or whatever. And I'm more frightened of letting it all slip and reaching sixty and finding I've done nothing. I was in for a penny, and I'd be in for £100,000. I decided I'd still go for it, but the most crucial of all, I'd do it to the fullest, not half-heartedly.'

He was, indeed, his father's son.

At the last minute he concluded a deal with another New Zealander, Murray Taylor, a former journalist who was running his own team. Paired with Paul Radisich, who is now a leading light in the British Touring Car Championship, he finally embarked on the great graduation. It was a competitive season, and a different sort of reality to face, for just as cars had initially been a culture shock, so he was to find F3 a different proposition to Formula Ford. A big lesson lay in store: everything to do with racing car dynamics had been a complete mystery to him until he drove that Ralt RT30.

'In Formula Ford it was just a case of balance and drive. If you got geed up you could drive faster. In F3 that just doesn't work. You can't physically drive a car quicker unless it's fully sorted.

'My mechanic Kevin Corin showed me how to learn and what I should be learning about, and Murray was good at helping me keep my self-confidence.'

Damon was honest enough to admit that his lack of knowledge and experience might have worked against him with Bennetts, who, though easygoing, placed a huge premium on driver feedback.

As the season progressed so did Damon, and though victory eluded him there were sufficient occasions upon which he was able to demonstrate speed and promise. For 1987 he was offered a pukka works drive with Intersport Racing, who enjoyed sponsorship from Cellnet. He had turned another corner.

That season he graduated with honours, winning the two overseas races in the British Championship, at Zandvoort in Holland and Spa-Francorchamps in Belgium, where later he would take Formula One laurels as well. With that full 1986 season behind him he had matured into a consistent challenger. Had Intersport been more fortunate and its TOM'S Toyota engines reached their development peak sooner, Hill and Donnelly might well have challenged Johnny Herbert for the title.

Martin Donnelly was Hill's team-mate in their Cellnet F3 days. On the occasion of the Cellnet Superprix at Knockhill in Scotland the pair had shared the front row of the grid, and Donnelly had gone on to win after Hill, equally anxious to succeed, had slid straight off on the first corner. Appropriately, perhaps, it was called Duffus (pronounced Duffer's) Dip. Racing folklore suggests that the following day

All three drivers atop the 1987 Spa F3 rostrum would graduate to F1, but Hill's Cellnet teammate Martin Donnelly would crash heavily, and friend Roland Ratzenberger would be killed at Imola in 1994, the same weekend as Senna.

both were given a dressing down and, temporarily, their P45s by Marketing Director Peter Waller. Jim Wright, who co-ordinated Cellnet's racing programme, remembers things slightly differently.

'I don't recall it that way, quite. They were both ticked off, but they weren't sacked as far as I know. But let's face it, they were up there effectively to do a demonstration, and for them virtually to collide and one to end up in the hedge was a bit stupid!'

Wright had been instrumental in Hill getting the Cellnet drive, for he had him at the top of his driver list after the EJR test in late 1985. 'He fitted Cellnet's requirements very well, and I believed in him as a driver. His first year of F3 wasn't bad, considering all the problems. He wasn't consistent, but he was good. With us, on his day he could be untouchable. Look at Zandvoort and Spa. And in 1988 he won in the wet at Thruxton, and then the race supporting the British GP, and he was totally dominant.'

AS THE SEASON PROGRESSED, SO DID HILL, AND THOUGH VICTORY ELUDED HIM THERE WERE SUFFICIENT OCCASIONS UPON WHICH HE WAS ABLE TO DEMONSTRATE SPEED AND PROMISE.

Hill raced at Monaco in his Formula Three Ralt in both 1987 and 1988, acquitting himself well on the streets upon which his father had reigned so often.

Later Donnelly graduated to Formula One with Lotus and showed great promise until a near-fatal accident in Spain curtailed his career in September 1990. He now runs his own junior formula racing team.

'Damon's determination has always showed,' he recalls. 'When we were together racing for Glenn in 1988, Cellnet sent us off with Jonathan Palmer to an RAF fitness course, because it not only wanted the best drivers, it also wanted the fittest. The assessments said that I was marginally fitter physically, but that Damon was more determined. He wanted things more. If I did fifty-one push-ups, then he had to do fifty-two. If I ran three miles, he had to run three and a half.

HE IMPRESSED PEOPLE ONCE AGAIN, BUT THE HIGHER YOU GET UP THE LADDER, THE GREATER THE PROBLEMS IN FINDING MONEY.

'You can still see that in his driving. He's got where he is through sheer perseverance. I don't think that he has the natural ability of Ayrton Senna or Alain Prost, but then nor did Nigel Mansell. But like Mansell, his determination can get him there. Nigel, for example, has that determination that can take any car – a Williams, a Ferrari or even a Pacific – and just wring everything out of it. But Senna had a knack of driving round problems in the car; I don't think that either Nigel or Damon have that ability.'

Hill and Donnelly had a reasonable working relationship, though both had the periods of paranoia that are an inevitable part of the racing driver's emotional hand baggage. 'When you have two strong drivers it can tend to divide a team,' says Wright. 'In 1987 Damon was a bit paranoid at times, but then Glenn was one of those people who got very, very upset when people crashed his cars – and Damon did that rather more than Martin.'

Hill stepped up to the final rung of the nursery ladder late in 1988 when he drove a Formula 3000 Lola for GA Motorsport at Zolder and Dijon, hopefully in readiness for an assault in 1989. He impressed people once

By 1988 Hill was firmly established within Formula Three, and earning good money as a Cellnet driver, but the lure of F3000 was always the next focus.

Japanese preferred him because of his background and his name. They knew more about him. It was hardly a top drive, but it was regular work and the perfect opportunity to learn.

'Even then I suppose I felt that the test drive route is the one realistic way for drivers, especially British drivers, with little or no sponsorship, to get into Formula One,' says Damon. 'The test route, or by trying to get yourself into a car, whatever it is. People have asked me why I wanted to drive that Footwork. Why did I want to drive such a heap of junk? And why did I want to drive the F1 Brabham subsequently? If you can't drive anything else, you've got to drive something, haven't you? If you stand still you're not going anywhere.

'At the end of 1989 the Cellnet thing had finished the year before. I had no sponsorship – not for want of trying, but it's just very difficult to get people in England interested for the sums of money you're talking about. It's very, very difficult here to get people to put money up for motor racing. So I decided whatever opportunity I get of driving a car, I'm going to have to make bloody good use of it because it might be the last chance. When I went to the first round of the European F3000 Championship at the beginning of 1989, having wanted to do it but been unable to find the money, I saw old Colin Bennett from CoBra and he said: "'Ere, do you wanna drive my car?" because he'd just started the European championship. And of course I said yes, because I hadn't got anything else to do. He gave me the opportunity of a few races

again, but the higher you get up the ladder, the greater the problems in finding money. It's like the way aerodynamic forces become multiplied by the square of a car's speed. Plenty of people were interested, but only if he could bring money. Hill had nothing like enough, but there was one lifeline. The Japanese company Footwork was running its own curiously named Mooncraft MC-041 chassis in the European F3000 Championship, using a British-based team headed by John Wickham. Footwork was also contesting its domestic F3000 series, and after a while it became clear that running Ukyo Katayama in both wasn't doing anyone any favours.

'Ukyo agreed to concentrate on Japan only,' says Wickham, 'so we needed to replace him. I'd known Perry McCarthy for some time and had been impressed with his ability, while I'd worked with Damon via TOM'S involvement with Intersport in supplying Toyota engines for F3. They were the two obvious candidates and we ran them at Snetterton.

'Perry was exciting and obviously totally committed. Russell corner was very quick in those days and he was frighteningly fast through there. Damon was as quick, but a bit more organised perhaps outside the car.'

In the end engineer Alan Langridge felt he would be happier working with Hill, and the

'I WAS KIND OF PICKING DRIVES, NOT THROUGH BRINGING ANY MONEY BUT BECAUSE PEOPLE THOUGHT I WAS CAPABLE AND THEY NEEDED SOMEBODY TO PUT IN THE CAR.'

in the British rounds for not very much money, and I think because of that I got the chance to drive Richard Lloyd Racing's Porsche at Le Mans. So I was kind of picking drives, not through bringing any money but because people thought I was capable and they needed somebody to put in the car. Then I got the chance to test the Footwork 3000 and I knew I wasn't going to turn that down if they offered me the chance of a drive. And it sort of went like that.'

Sharing the Porsche 962 at Le Mans with veteran David Hobbs and Steven Andskar, Damon had a slim chance of matching his father's 1972 success for Matra, but the engine broke around two-thirds distance. Shortly afterwards, the Footwork opportunity rescued him from obscurity.

'Damon worked well with Alan,' Wickham remembers. 'They had a good rapport on chassis set-up and did some limited development work, although there was nothing they could do about the car's aerodynamic shortcomings. But he qualified for virtually every race.'

And his performances nearly led there and then to his first F1 drive.

'At the end of the year the future was uncertain,' Wickham continues. 'At the time I wasn't aware of Footwork's immediate desire to go F1, which they subsequently did with the Arrows team. So we put forward four proposals. The first was stay in F3000 another year and then go F1. The second was to buy an F1 team. The third was to race the Footwork car which Mooncraft in Japan was developing. And the fourth was to take an updated version of de-

Famous names. In his F3 heyday Hill poses with Paul Stewart (son of Jackie), the late Paul Warwick (brother of Derek) and David Brabham (son of Sir Jack).

signer George Ryton's Euro Brun ER189 chassis and use it for F1.

'Obviously Damon would have driven the F3000 car, and if the Ryton deal had come off he'd have had a good chance of driving that. But the easier option proved to be Arrows.'

By this time Damon had actually driven two F1 cars. In 1987 he had a brief run in his father's old GH2 which had been down at the National Motor Museum in Beaulieu – 'It was quite fun, but an eye-opener. It had around 420bhp and very little grip compared to the cars I'd become used to driving.' And in December that year he was also invited to try a Benetton B187 at Paul Ricard. 'He surprised me how quick he was,' admitted Peter Col-lins, now Managing Director of Team Lotus but at that time Benetton's team manager. 'He did a good, solid job and, to be honest, did better than Martin Don-nelly had when we'd tried him at Estoril.'

Herbert, however, had done better still in the car at Brands Hatch – Nigel Mansell had been prompted at the time to enquire, '*Who* is driving that?' – and it was Herbert who Collins backed for the future.

This latest chance of F1 had been slim, but there would be others. Hill had no doubt why they came along. 'If I hadn't done all those things, just driven whatever I had the chance to drive and tried to make the best of it, I wouldn't have got the Middlebridge 3000 drive,' he insists. That came along for 1990, and helped him to establish a reputation for speed and the ability to lead races that would directly interest Frank Williams.

Formula 3000 is the grown-up version of Formula Three. Again, the cars are similar to their F1 brethren, but they are more powerful than F3s. They use three-litre engines (some of them developed from the Cosworth DFV which used to rule the roost in Formula One after its dramatic introduction in 1967), restricted to around 450bhp. They are heavier

> HILL'S CARS MIGHT HAVE BEEN FRAGILE, BUT HE WAS FAST, AND THAT WAS CRUCIAL. IT CONVINCED FRANK WILLIAMS THAT HE COULD LEAD MOTOR RACES.

than F3 cars, and the races are longer, too, placing greater demands on a driver's physical fitness. Historically the European Championship has always been very closely fought, and though the cars are not as fast as Formula One and do not generate anything like the same aerodynamic downforce and cornering load, getting the best out of them does require a very high level of skill. They therefore provide an apposite final stepping stone for aspiring Grand Prix drivers.

Damon failed to qualify the team's Lola T90/50 for the season-opener at Donington because the cars weren't fully sorted, but led the next race at Silverstone. He would have won, too, if his engine hadn't cut out. He took pole position three times, and led five races.

His best result, though, was a second at Brands Hatch. Those were the only points he scored all season.

The following year there was sponsorship from Barclay cigarettes in a complicated sub-deal between Middlebridge and EJR, but the Lola was not as competitive as the Reynard chassis. Despite having drivers of the calibre of Hill, Vincenzo Sospiri, Allan McNish and Marco Apicella, the T91/50 didn't win any races, although Damon bullied his way to the front at Brands and kept faster cars at bay for a while. When he switched to a Reynard for the season finale at Nogaro, however, he was immediately back on the pace. Running standard 'pump' fuel, rather than the more exotic brews that teams such as Pacific Racing and Il Barone

Rampante could afford, he was able to hang on to the latter's Alessandro Zanardi (who now races IndyCars). He might have given him a closer run for second place if his own team-mate, Sospiri, hadn't been overcome by petulance and driven him off the track on two occasions. He finished third.

Ray Boulter worked as an engineer with Middlebridge, and recalls Hill as an even-tempered individual, no matter what disappointments he had to face. 'And there were a lot in 1990, with all the electrical problems that we had. He coped very well, and perhaps that came with being a bit older than most drivers, more mature mentally. He dealt with that really well. He didn't throw all his toys out of the pram. Well, not very often, anyway!

At Silverstone's International Trophy F3000 race in 1990, Hill led Scottish driver Allan McNish in his similar Lola, and was set for victory when the engine cut out. McNish won.

Throughout 1990 Hill's handling of the Middlebridge Lola T90/50 confirmed him as a man to watch. He led several races, but usually succumbed to electrical trouble.

'In 1991 the car wasn't so good, but we were reasonably competitive and he generally maintained an even keel. But I found that it takes a lot of getting to know him. He's very introverted until you get to know him well, and then he opens up and you see a whole different side to him. That came across in the car, too. But he's quite forceful when he needs to be. He wasn't backwards in coming forward.'

His F3000 results were similar to those Nigel Mansell scored in the early years of his career. They were patchy and didn't look too good on paper, but those who knew racing could see something valuable beneath the dull external veneer. Hill's cars might have been fragile, but he was fast, and that was crucial. It convinced Frank Williams that he could lead motor races. When he eventually signed him as his team's test driver – and then later as Prost's racing partner for 1993 – Frank did so because he was quick, and he fitted into the team. Effectively,

Damon Hill had made his own luck. He had made something happen instead of sitting about waiting for things to turn up.

It took Mansell some time testing with Lotus before he had the chance to set quick lap times, and it was the same when Hill started his work with Williams. 'The first couple of tests I did were with the TG3, I think, the semi-automatic gearbox, bolted on the back of the FW13B chassis. I did a day's running . . . Well, I didn't do much running, actually, because it kept breaking! But the moment we started running the FW14 I got a good go. It was Imola where I took over from Riccardo Patrese and was first able to really push it. That was in the early part of 1991. Because he had done good lap times, and I was within a second or so of them, I felt that that was the first time I'd been allowed to push the car. I'd never been to Imola before, so I was quite pleased with that. The car was in a condition that required me to

drive it quickly, otherwise they wouldn't have found anything out.'

He discovered that there was a great deal to find out in comparison with his F3000 experience. 'There are far more variables in F1, a lot more things to take on board. You just don't do any development in 3000, to speak of. You don't have to look after the tyres necessarily; they never blister. Within reason you run what you brung in 3000.

'In Formula One, especially testing with Williams, you've got brake people turning up with new kit to try, you've got an engine manufacturer constantly making changes to its power unit, mapping, different camshafts, different this, that and the other. You never go out with the car in the same condition, so the workload is much higher and the whole thing's a constant learning curve. You have to have your wits about you.'

Damon certainly had his where they belonged. To get the Williams test drive, at Wright's suggestion and with his help, he had produced a document for Frank illustrating not only what he had done on the track in terms of results, but also which drivers then currently racing in F1 he had beaten at various stages of his career. It was a belt-and-braces operation that was ultimately to prove highly successful.

'That was how I got the Williams test, which also came about because Mark Blundell left when he got the Brabham F1 drive for 1991. I mean, if you look at my c.v. it was pretty miserable, really, by comparison to a lot of these guys, who win Vauxhall Lotus, who win Formula Three, Formula 3000. But if I'd had the backing earlier on I think I might have had one of those titles.' He paused for a moment, perhaps recalling the old arguments and fearing he might sound as if he was whingeing. 'But then I'm not complaining about anything.'

Indeed he wasn't. For the first time in a long while in December 1991, he and his wife Georgie had the luxury of being able to enjoy Christmas knowing that he had a job for the next season. He wasn't yet racing in F1, but his foot was firmly in the door.

Man in a hurry. At Brands Hatch in 1991 Hill burst through to snatch the lead into Paddock Bend, but the Reynards outclassed his Lola and he finished sixth.

4

THE SUBLIME AND THE RIDICULOUS

WHEN DAMON HILL MADE HIS GRAND
PRIX DEBUT IT WAS NOT WITH WILLIAMS
BUT WITH THE STRUGGLING BRABHAM
TEAM. BUT AS POLITICS TOOK THEIR
TOLL ON NIGEL MANSELL'S RELATIONSHIP
WITH WILLIAMS, FATE CONSPIRED TO
CREATE ONE OF THE FEW FAIRY TALES OF
MODERN TIMES IN FORMULA ONE.

At the start of 1992, Damon Hill had reached a vital crossroads in his career. At the time only Nigel Mansell had successfully turned the role of test driver at Lotus into that of a regular drive in races, so Damon was under no illusions as he continued the similar task at Williams. Thus began a year of contrasts.

Most weeks he would clamber into the car with which Mansell was crushing his World Championship opposition and pound round in lonely test sessions, while on alternate weekends he would attempt to qualify a lamentably slow Brabham-Judd for races. It was a feat he managed only twice, and in each of his two Grands Prix he finished many laps behind Mansell. It was his year of great hunger.

While Williams was setting the technological standards for Formula One that season, and Damon was helping it to develop its wares, the Brabham team was in its death throes, struggling along with an uncompetitive update of the previous year's BT60 design and saddled with debts that demanded a constant juggling act from Dennis Nursey, the man charged with running things on behalf of Kohji Nakauchi, who owned not only Brabham but the Middlebridge team for whom Hill had raced in F3000.

Brabham had started the season with the Belgian driver Eric van de Poele and the first woman to try her hand at Formula One for a decade, the fiery Italian Giovanna Amati. A former amour of Benetton team chief Flavio Briatore and another graduate from F3 and F3000, she would achieve rather more enduring fame off-track as Niki Lauda's romantic interest. By the fifth race of the season it was clear not only that she was unlikely to qualify but also that her sponsorship money was not going to arrive. Meanwhile, it was also obvious to Damon Hill that his hopes of continuing in F3000 with Alolique, a team born out of Middlebridge, were not going to be realised.

'We were strapped for cash,' recalls Ray Boulter, who was now working at Brabham, 'and Giovanna hadn't paid and it was fairly clear that she wasn't going to. The team felt that if we were going to run someone for free, then it might as well be someone in whom we had faith.'

From yet another spell of enforced racing unemployment, Hill was summoned back into action. He failed to qualify at the Spanish GP, and again in Imola, Monaco, Canada and

Climbing the ladder. After all the tribulations of 1990, Hill started the '91 season as Williams' official test driver.

France, but at Silverstone for the British GP he scraped into twenty-sixth – last – place on the grid. He finished the event, too, in sixteenth place, four laps down on eventual winner Nigel Mansell. At the finish, amid scenes of utter hysteria, he came close to running over the hundreds of Mansell fans as they flooded the track to embrace their victorious hero.

Two years later, when a more dignified crowd saluted the next British victor of the British GP, his name would be Damon Hill.

The Brabham failed him again in Germany, where he missed the cut, but after countless dramas he scraped into the Hungarian race a fortnight later, as Boulter relates.

'He did a blinding job for us there. Because of our continuing financial problems our trucks hadn't left until Tuesday night and they only arrived in the paddock in Hungary at midnight on Thursday. Eric had left to join the Fondmetal team, so we were down to just one car. Then on Friday we were restricted in the amount of revs we could use on the Judd V10 engines, because of our financial situation with John Judd's Engine Developments company. Judd himself was in America, and because we hadn't paid the bills by Saturday morning he asked us not to run. Meanwhile, as Damon sat on the sidelines, Dennis was trying to reach agreement with John, and his man on the spot, Stan Hall, was very helpful. We missed all of free practice on Saturday morning, and as second qualifying approached in the afternoon John finally agreed to let us participate.

At Barcelona in 1992 Hill sits awaiting the start of his first-ever F1 free practice session with the Brabham BT60B.

Despite sterling efforts, Hill could not persuade the uncompetitive Brabham into the 1992 San Marino Grand Prix at Imola.

'Then Damon went out and wrote one car off by putting a big hole in the chassis over a kerb, so he jumped into the second BT60B and came very close to qualifying with it, but we were still only allowed to use 10,750 rpm, which wasn't very good. I pleaded with Stan to let us have a few more revs, closer to 12,000, because Damon was so close to getting in, and he gave us three laps with more. I pushed for five.

'Well, Damon went out, did his final run, ran with almost normal revs and got into the race. He wasn't even last, but twenty-fifth out of twenty-six.

'We'd been using the phone in the Lotus motorhome in all our negotiations, so Peter Collins was aware of all our problems, and when we got in he came down to congratulate us and it was as if we'd won. Then we were brought back down to earth when Judd's said, 'Well, what are you going to do for an engine for the race?' That brought a whole new set of problems, but in the end we did race. Damon was slow, but he brought the car home in eleventh place. When you look at what Simtek and Pacific did in 1994, that wasn't so bad.'

The situation at Brabham called for a special kind of driver, just as it had at Footwork in 1989. Not just any driver would have fitted the bill. The team needed someone who was calm and analytical, who didn't get flustered or excited too easily, who wouldn't scream and shout, and who would get his head down and do the job without complaint. Moreover, one who could appreciate that things were being run on a shoestring, but remain totally committed.

'We weren't ever using any parts that had gone beyond their operational life,' Boulter stresses. 'Damon only ever asked me once if the car was safe, and I told him just that. I also told him that if it hadn't been, we wouldn't have run it.

'He always gave his best and his aim was to finish. And we did finish every race we started; it's just that we didn't start many! It's difficult to judge him on those performances because of all the factors involved, but it gives an idea about some points of his character. He was always a gentleman, amiable to everybody. Not a superstar, but then in that situation it was diffi-

cult to be. He did extremely well in difficult circumstances, and it was all good experience for him.'

The Hungarian GP was Brabham's last outing, as the financial sword of Damocles inevitably fell thereafter. It was also the race in which Nigel Mansell clinched his World Championship, but in which his relationship with Williams finally fell apart.

Formula One is a highly political business at the best of times, and all season such issues had been running high at Williams. Mansell was dominating the races, and in Mexico had turned down an extremely lucrative offer from the team to agree terms for 1993. Since then it had become crystal clear to him that even if he were to stay, Williams was hell-bent on signing his old adversary and former Ferrari team-mate Alain Prost, and this proved too much for him. Accusing the team of betrayal, he dug his feet in for more money at precisely the time that the bottom temporarily fell out of the driver market, thanks in part to Senna offering in

Hungary to drive the Williams, 'for nothing'.

That, of course, was a bit of clever gamesmanship from the Brazilian, who enjoyed a well-founded reputation for knowing the precise value of a dollar, and it destabilised Mansell further.

As the Briton's most successful season drew to a close it became clear that, World Championship notwithstanding, he would not be staying at Williams. Suddenly, as Mansell headed off for a new start with Newman-Haas Racing on the American IndyCar circuit, the best seat in the business was available. You didn't need genius IQ to work out that Damon Hill was one of the prime candidates to fill it.

He would spend a nail-biting winter pushing desperately hard to join Alain Prost in the race team, and he was backed up by the technical group at Williams which had no doubts about his ability, despite his patchy racing background. But other established stars such as Mika Hakkinen, Johnny Herbert and Martin Brundle were all very much in the running as

Though Hill desperately wanted to succeed where his father had been the king, Monaco in 1992 would also prove barren.

Brabham's new colour scheme signified nothing more than a revised image. After finishing sixteenth in Britain, the team again failed to qualify in Germany.

Hard trier. In Hungary, where Mansell clinched his World Championship, Hill hustled the Brabham to eleventh place. Better things lay ahead.

well. It was certainly not a foregone conclusion who Frank would pick.

On the positive side there were factors working in Hill's favour. Peter Collins was reluctant to release either Herbert or Hakkinen without serious compensation and eventually frightened Williams away, while in the background the French Ligier team was expressing very firm interest in signing Damon for 1993. He thus walked a tightrope. If he didn't get the Williams he had something, albeit a drive that came nowhere near close to what Williams could offer in terms of competitiveness. He had to be very careful not to put that feeling into words, for fear of alienating the people who could provide his 'safety net'.

Eventually, just before Christmas, Frank Williams gave Hill the best Christmas present he could have asked for. For reasons that have

still to be disclosed, he changed his mind about signing Brundle at the last moment, just as a deal had been agreed, and opted for Hill. The drive was his.

By any standard it was a fairy tale in a sport that shuns sentiment, but Williams's decision was the product of gut feeling and hard logic.

As the winter agony subsided Damon settled down to the role of testing in preparation for his first full season of F1. But the memory of that limbo period remained vivid. 'The worst part,' he admitted, 'was the thought that I might end up with nothing. I was warm about the Ligier chance, but on the one hand, with no disrespect to Ligier, you've got the best drive in Formula One and then the chance of a good drive in Formula One. I thought, If I hang on for the best drive and the Ligier drive, Ligier can't wait much longer, and I stood a chance of losing both. And I thought, Well, what do you do? If I'd plumped for second best, how would I feel if Frank turned round and said, "Why didn't you wait? I would have given you a try with Williams if you'd just waited." But I daren't try and put any pressure on him at the time.

'The worst thing was waiting, not being able to do anything. I was absolutely fine when I was testing at Estoril, because I knew at least I was in command of my own destiny, to some degree. But the limbo period was awful.'

Williams's faith in signing Hill, with only those two Grands Prix behind him, surprised some observers, particularly since it meant turning down the established Brundle. It was not something done lightly, either, which perhaps made comprehension all the harder for Brundle. What did not influence Frank at all, and it is telling, is the fact that Damon was the son of Graham Hill. From an early stage Damon had established a solid relationship with Patrick Head, and he readily acknowledged the help he had to settle in as tester.

'He was very good with me, because whilst he made it clear that I needed to do the job in the car, in the early days he was always very encouraging and gave me room, if you like, to make the odd mistake and to learn the ropes. When I first started in the test he said, "Just build up

very gently. We're not expecting you to go and break the lap record. We just want to get the work done." So he made it easy for me to start with.

'When I first went there I was surprised at the sheer amount of work Williams had to get through, and the speed at which it works. The people there don't hang around. What they'll do is do a test, they'll get an impression from it, they'll get data and then they'll go on to the next thing. And then maybe the thing you've just tested might come back a month later and they'll test again, but by doing that, instead of just faffing around and sort of umming and erring, they get work done. It's a product of Patrick's methods, his modus operandi. He likes to make a decision and get on with the next thing.'

Following Williams's decision to sign him, Damon's answerphone worked overtime, and became a valuable buffer so that he and his family could enjoy a modicum of peace.

'The bugger is watching what you say to people,' he said with a laugh. 'At the moment I've got to be very careful that I don't appear to come across as an upstart. Although I'm very confident of my own abilities I'm also aware that I've done absolutely nothing in a Formula One context and people are asking all these questions about how I'm going to get on with Prost.'

He asked the Fleet Street writers not to expect too much of him too soon, saying, 'I don't want to make any wild claims at all, it's unrealistic. To expect me to sort of leap in and take on the guy who's won more races than anyone else, and make him look silly – it's just not going to happen. It's far more difficult, Formula One, than that. And I've got no illusions.'

In the weeks building up to Kyalami he continued testing and his physical preparation. 'When I first drove the Williams I must admit that I was completely stuffed,' he confessed.

> 'WHEN I FIRST DROVE THE WILLIAMS I MUST ADMIT THAT I WAS COMPLETELY STUFFED.'

Wise heads. Hill and Williams's Technical Director Patrick Head have formed an alliance based on mutual respect for the other's talents.

glumly alongside Mansell, as the latter was presented with the Sports Personality of the Year award, but his morose expression had nothing to do with the fact that he knew he had the drive at Williams and was obliged to bottle it up. He was bottling up something rather more personal. 'I was actually dying to go to the loo! I knew I should have gone before everything started!'

There were many ironies that evening, not the least that Mansell was the last tester-turned-racer, and Damon was now preparing to take over his very seat. But there was another, for earlier in the year, around Monaco time, Hill had been approached to stand in for the injured Mario Andretti at Newman-Haas. It didn't come off in the end, but here was Mansell now headed for that very team.

The South African Grand Prix kicked off the new season at the Kyalami track near Johannesburg, where Williams fielded a brace of FW15Cs for its new driver and his new partner. For Hill there would now be no excuses. He was wholly familiar with the car, if not the venue, and was expected to perform, while few really anticipated that Prost's 1992 sabbatical would in any way have affected his level of performance. Once qualifying was over it was indeed clear that the French genius had lost nothing, as he took pole position ahead of Senna's McLaren, Schu-macher's Benetton . . . and Damon Hill. The latter's was a terrific performance, but one that was forgotten within seconds of the start.

Prost was slow away, and as Senna shot to the fore Hill found himself almost reluctantly thrust into second place. It lasted as far as the second corner, where he lost downforce on his

'It's difficult to train for it. You can prepare as much as you like, but only doing it really helps.' He paused. 'To be fair, that's a bit of an exaggeration; I wasn't as bad as I thought I would be first time out. There was a lot more steering load and g-load than I was used to, but I think I coped quite well and that was partly because in 1991 when I raced with EJR in 3000, we did more miles before the start of the season than we did the whole of the year before! And then I did quite a bit of testing throughout the year for Eddie, so I'd done quite a few miles before I got the drive with Williams. I think that 3000 is a very good preparatory formula in that sense. I think the performance level now is high. Hakkinen has done brilliantly to come straight from Formula Three to Formula One. Not many people can do that.'

It was interesting that Damon singled out the Finn, for in the early races of 1994 their relations would cool, especially after their brush in the Pacific GP and then their startline collision in Monte Carlo.

'There isn't a lot of difference between a slow Formula One car and an F3000 car,' he continued. 'The real difference lies between a slow Formula One car and a fast Formula One car like the Williams, which is almost as big as from 3000 to Formula One. It's about six seconds a lap.'

At the 1992 BBC Sports Review Hill sat rather

THE WILLIAMS SPUN, WAS MERCIFULLY AVOIDED BY THE REST OF THE FIELD, AND HILL RESUMED A CHASTENED ELEVENTH.

Interpreting the information relayed by the timing system, and acting upon it, is a crucial factor in finding traffic-free laps during qualifying sessions.

car's front wings by running too close to the McLaren. The Williams spun, was mercifully avoided by the rest of the field, and Hill resumed a chastened eleventh. Racing Lesson Number One had come the hard way, and would be compounded a little later when an over-anxious Alessandro Zanardi collided with him during an ill-starred overtaking attempt and forced both into retirement.

The Brazilian Grand Prix on Senna's home ground brought better fortune, for, as Prost spun into retirement in a sudden downpour, Damon came through to uphold Williams's honour with second place behind his Brazilian ad-

Pupil and master. Hill learned an immense amount not only about racecraft but also about speed with style, from his 1993 partnership with four-time champion Alain Prost.

versary. He thus scored his first six World Championship points and proved that even in extremely trying conditions he could keep a cool head.

Better still, he had overtaken Senna early in the event to run second to Prost, and had actually led for five laps at the mid-point after Prost's misfortune. Senna had then used his vast experience to gain the lead, but Hill refused to give up the chase, even after a big slide had lost him ground just regained, and it was only in the closing stages that he finally decided to settle for his best-ever finish.

'I can relax a bit and yet on the other hand,' he said afterwards, 'I have to raise my game even more and push harder.'

At the one-off European Grand Prix at Donington Park, he again coped well with pressure as the track conditions see-sawed maddeningly between wet, drying and wet. As Senna produced one of the most commanding performances of his career, Hill and Prost scurried time and again for the pits to change from wet-weather tyres to treadless slicks and back in his wake. Both were handicapped by the poor quality of their gearboxes' downchanges, which made life even more difficult as, together, they made thirteen stops. Despite all this, Damon was again second, Alain third.

At Imola he briefly led again before succumbing to a frenetic battle for the lead between Prost and Senna. When he encountered a spongey brake pedal going into the Tosa hairpin on lap twenty-one he plunged into igno-

enth F1 event), the Spanish Grand Prix at Barcelona a year after his pukka début, he narrowly missed out on pole position as Prost called on all his speed and experience. It was another indication of his potential. In the race, too, he was on course for the first win of his career, having grabbed the lead at the start. Though Prost subsequently took it from him on lap eleven, Hill remained close enough to launch a serious counter-attack by the thirty-lap mark. He was right behind his team-mate, looking for the opportunity to overtake without putting them both at risk, when his engine broke a piston with twenty-five laps left.

Vibrations had made it a tough race for Prost, who said afterwards, 'Damon was pushing me a lot. If he had been able to stay like this, as fast as this, I would have been in trouble for sure.'

When Prost was unfairly penalised for an alleged jump start in Monaco, Senna was home and dry. But again Hill underlined his burgeoning reputation with a strong second place, despite an assault at the Loews hairpin when Gerhard Berger somewhat rashly attempted to squeeze by in his Ferrari. Both cars spun, but only Hill managed to restart and carried on to finish runner-up on the day when Senna's sixth – and final – Monaco victory finally took him to a new all-time record. Prior to that he had been equal with Graham Hill's tally of five.

'I have to say, if my father had been around

minious retirement. Afterwards he was summoned to appear before Senna to answer accusations about his driving technique. The Brazilian was extremely miffed that this newcomer should employ 'aggressive' tactics to keep him behind, and wanted to discuss things.

Hill listened politely as Senna ranted, and then replied that he had merely based his own tactics on those he had seen Ayrton apply, and, without even raising his voice, won the psychological encounter. 'There wasn't much he could say after that,' he said with a smile.

So far he had indicated that he had the speed and aggression to lead races, and the coolness to finish them well up in the points. What's more, his qualifying times weren't far off Prost's. In the fifth race of the season (his sev-

Faith rewarded. Once Frank Williams had taken the gamble to give his test driver a race seat, Hill did everything to repay the debt.

At Monaco in 1993 Ayrton Senna broke Graham Hill's record of wins, but Damon did all he could to defend family honour with second place.

he would have been the first to congratulate Ayrton,' Damon said.

Canada yielded third place after he led briefly off the line, but later lost time due to confusion during his routine tyre change.

The French Grand Prix at Magny-Cours was a showcase event for Renault, who flew in countless guests in expectation not just of more Williams-Renault domination, but of victory by a French driver. For the first time in the season it was suggested that team orders were dictating a victory for Alain, the deal being, it was said, that if Damon played ball in France he would be allowed to win a week later in Britain, assuming of course that no other team emerged to spoil that plan. Whether the various political machinations got to him Damon was not saying, but he was sufficiently wound up to take his first pole position, and in the race he was ostentatiously on Prost's gearbox at the finish as they swept across the line in Renault's desired order. They were only three-tenths of a second apart, and that represented the margin by which he had been denied his first victory. Insiders at Williams made no bones about Re-nault's request that the junior driver play a supporting role.

THE SCENE WAS THUS SET FOR THE BRITISH GRAND PRIX, AND THE HILL FAMILY CROSSED ITS FINGERS, FOR THIS WAS THE ONE RACE THAT GRAHAM HILL HAD NEVER BEEN ABLE TO WIN.

The scene was thus set for the British Grand Prix, and as the national media went into overdrive at the prospect of a home win, the Hill family crossed its fingers, for this was the one race that Graham Hill had never been able to win. He had led many British Grands Prix – and in 1960 had come within seven laps of victory before spinning as a result of fading brakes and succumbing to pressure from Jack Brabham. Somehow, victory for Damon would lay a family ghost.

The redoubtable television commentator Murray Walker was just congratulating him on taking pole position when Prost beat his time, but in the race Hill was firmly in control when the safety car was momentarily deployed while a broken car was moved. The moment the track went 'green' again Hill made a huge ef-

Stung by the obvious team orders mandated by Renault Sport, Hill took his first F1 pole position at Magny-Cours for the 1993 French Grand Prix.

(Left) With eighteen laps of the 1993 British Grand Prix to run, Hill's hopes went up in smoke due to engine failure as he was leading Prost. (Opposite) Damon had made the perfect start at Silverstone, as Senna burst through to beat Prost into Copse Corner.

Deflated hopes. At Hockenheim the German Grand Prix, like the British, had been in the bag until tyre failure sent Hill walking back to the pits. Prost won again.

fort to pull away again from Prost, and felt he was in control when his engine suddenly erupted with eighteen laps left. The fairy tale had been denied.

'I wasn't so much deflated as angry – really angry. You feel really cheated because you didn't get the opportunity to see for yourself whether you had it in you to do the finals laps at such a hard pace,' he said.

Incredibly, fate was to strike at him again in Germany a fortnight later where, after Prost had run into trouble and been given an unmerited stop-and-go penalty, he found himself leading with three laps remaining. Prost had recovered but was no longer a threat, and Hill had been given the OK to retain his position, despite Alain's need for as many Championship points as possible. Hill was on his penultimate lap, but as we checked our charts he was overdue. As Prost sped by, now firmly in the lead, the blue and yellow Williams with the number zero on its flanks crept slowly into the stadium,

High tension. His own qualifying runs over, Hill, together with Frank Williams and Patrick Head, watches the monitors anxiously to see how quickly Prost is going.

Hockenheim this was definitely over and done'

But the hat trick of victories finally came. The first was made easier by Prost's engine stalling at the start of the formation lap for the Hungarian Grand Prix, obliging him to start from the back of the grid. That day, Damon Hill drove faultlessly – especially whenever he went by a spectating Senna, whose McLaren had retired out on the track. Fate finally smiled upon him as he became the first second-generation driver ever to win a Grand Prix since the World Championship began in 1950.

'It wasn't until I picked up Monday's newspaper that I really began to believe I had won my

With Prost forced to start from the back, Hill took a confident lead in Hungary and would never be overtaken as he headed en route to his first Grand Prix win.

its left rear Goodyear tyre deflated. By the time he reached the pit entry the rubber had been destroyed completely, and the car spun before beaching itself on a kerb. Hill, his face set but his temper and emotions under complete control, marched back to the pits for the second time in succession as Prost took the victory that ought to have been his. It would be the Frenchman's last.

'This was much, much worse than Silverstone,' he said. 'In the British Grand Prix there was still some way to go to the finish. At

first Grand Prix,' he admitted. 'You can't fully believe you can do it until you've actually done it. But now that I've won for the first time, I know it's possible.'

When Mansell won his first Grand Prix at Brands Hatch in 1985 he immediately followed it up with another in South Africa. So it proved with Hill. In Hungary the pressure had been to maintain his concentration while running alone after his main rivals had retired early on. At Spa it was to withstand a fierce final onslaught from Schumacher and Prost on the fastest circuit in the calendar. This he did in great style, and he then went one better than Mansell by taking the Italian Grand Prix at Monza too, after inheriting the lead when Prost's engine broke.

The media made much fuss about 'from zero to hero' and his chances now of catching Prost in the Championship chase, but in typical fashion Hill simply got his head down and concentrated on the job in hand. At Estoril for the Portuguese Grand Prix he was again on pole, but this time it was his turn to start at the back when the engine refused to fire up. This was where Schumacher scored his second victory, where Prost took the second place he needed to clinch his fourth world title but confirmed his plans to retire, and where Damon fought back to finish third. It was also where his own title aspirations finally died.

In the rain of Suzuka he was only fourth in the Japanese Grand Prix, but in the Australian finale he chased brilliantly after Prost. He spun in the wet, and the two of them finished second

Happiness is... As Prost ponders his enigmatic race in Belgium in 1993, Schumacher douses Hill after the Englishman's second consecutive victory.

Rarefied company. The competitiveness of the Williams-Renault regularly brought Hill wheel-to-wheel with Ayrton Senna during 1993, before their brief partnership the following season.

and third, a long way behind a Senna who was having another of his Day of Days performances in his last outing for McLaren.

By the end of 1993 Damon Hill was thus not just the seasoned veteran of a further sixteen races; he was the victor of three of them – in succession – and the moral victor of at least two more. He finished third in the World Championship behind the two greatest drivers then racing, Prost and Senna, and had won his

spurs the hard way. By any standard it had been a wildly successful first full season. You had to go back to the Swiss driver Clay Regazzoni in 1970 to find anyone else who had challenged so well in his first full year, and even Regga only took one victory.

Moreover, he had fitted in well at Williams, as his mechanic Les Jones recalls. 'Before he arrived everybody on the test team spoke very highly of him. He was very intelligent, the feed-

If Hill had been lucky when Prost stalled in Hungary, the tables were turned in Portugal, when a dead engine wasted his second pole position. He drove through to third place.

back from Patrick was that everybody rated him. Then he came along and, like most Grand Prix drivers, I suppose, it's a big learning curve. But he acted very maturely, buckled down behind Alain and gave him a run for his money.'

The greatest challenge lay ahead, however, for Prost was headed for retirement and Frank Williams had finally achieved his long-held ambition to sign Ayrton Senna. Damon's hand of aces was now full. In the past he had been stacked up against Mansell and then Prost. Now he would face the third great driver of the last decade, the one the majority of observers felt was the most ruthless of them all.

Though he had undoubtedly justified his drive with Williams and made every use of the opportunity, the very fact that Hill had made his own luck stuck in the craw of his detractors. Now they rubbed their hands and predicted that Senna would take him apart.

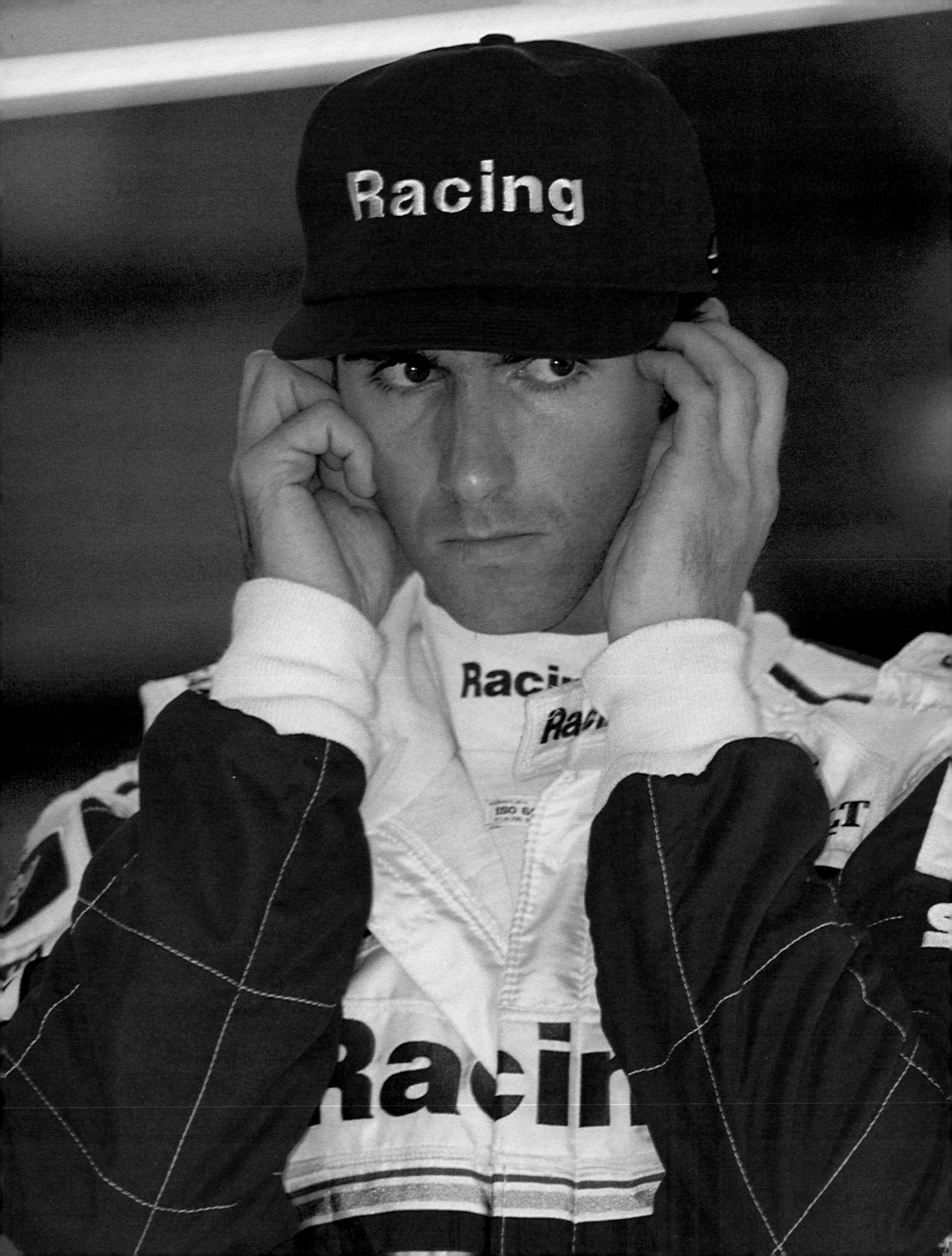
Racing

5

TRIUMPH AND TRAGEDY

NOBODY COULD POSSIBLY HAVE PREDICTED
THE AWFUL TURN THAT THE 1994 SEASON
WOULD TAKE AT THE SAN MARINO GRAND
PRIX. WITH THE DEATH OF AYRTON SENNA,
THE SPORT WAS THROWN INTO TURMOIL,
AND DAMON HILL SUDDENLY FELT THE
WEIGHT AND RESPONSIBILITY OF LEADING
ONE OF THE GREATEST TEAMS THRUST
UPON HIS SHOULDERS.

Nineteen ninety-four was going to be the greatest test of Damon Hill. But if his detractors expected him to be annihilated, his supporters relished the prospect of his stubborn refusal to be beaten, and prepared themselves to watch him fight his corner. Hill himself was outwardly relaxed about his team-mate, and simply pointed out that in his F1 career he had had the three best drivers of the time as his partners. As the media probed for his reaction to Senna and his renowned psychological destruction of team-mates, he replied, 'What do you think he's going to do, put me in a Vulcan mind grip?'

Prior to the first race it had largely been assumed that the Williams-Renault team, resplendent in the blue and white livery of Rothmans after the withdrawal of Camel and Canon, would simply take up where it had left off the previous season, especially as its greatest threat was now part of the team.

Controversial and bitterly opposed changes in the technical regulations had now outlawed the active suspension, traction control and power brakes that had helped to make the FW15Cs such formidable weapons, but it would be the same for all of the top teams and Williams remained the most organised, for Ferrari was still in turmoil and McLaren was now at the beginning of a new alliance with Peugeot, on the latter's Formula One début. Only Benetton was ready with an evolution of its 1993 car powered by a new Ford V8 engine, but though Michael Schumacher was expected to be very quick, most observers regarded it as a foregone conclusion that Senna would steamroller his way to a fourth World Championship.

It thus came as a rude shock when it became apparent that the German and his team had taken the lead in the pace-setting stakes. In the opening race in Brazil Senna took his fifty-ninth pole position and led initially, but after a faster fuel stop Schumacher took the lead and held it to the finish. To rub the message home, Senna uncharacteristically spun off in the closing stages while trying to keep up, leaving Damon to finish a distant second.

Refuelling during races had been reintroduced for 1994, necessitating fresh strategies from the teams. Within minutes of the start of the race it was clear to Williams that Hill's one-stop policy was not the way to go, but even that was of little consolation. Senna, like Schumacher, had gone for two fuel stops, and still had been beaten. The Williams FW16, it seemed, was a nervous package in comparison to the Benetton B194.

The remote TI Circuit near Aida in Japan, built on the whim of a wealthy enthusiast, hosted the next event, and there Benetton continued to hold sway. This time Schumacher made a lightning start to lead, but as Senna was slow away from pole position and had to brake hard in the first corner to avoid Schumacher, his Williams was rammed off the track by Mika Hakkinen,

At Estoril early in 1994, during the Rothmans-Williams launch, Hill and Senna began the uneasy process of forming a working relationship, neither knowing just how little time they had.

who had taken over his role of pace-setter at McLaren. Hill, too, would suffer at the Finn's hands, rejoining in ninth place after a spin. 'I tried to go up the inside at a particularly difficult place,' he said. 'Mika closed the door on me and I spun.' The corner where this happened, Revolver, had seen both he and Senna spin during qualifying. Damon had worked back to second, at one stage getting to within thirty-five seconds of Schumacher, but then his transmission failed on the fiftieth lap of eighty-three. Already the season was turning into a nightmare, but nothing could prepare Formula One for the events of the San Marino Grand Prix at Imola over the first May Bank Holiday weekend.

In qualifying the young Brazilian Rubens Barrichello was lucky to survive virtually unhurt after a heavy shunt in his Jordan on the Friday morning, and then on Saturday afternoon the likeable Austrian newcomer Roland

Ratzenberger died in a high-speed accident that befell his Simtek. He was the first F1 driver to be killed since Elio de Angelis in 1986, and his death cast a terrible pall over the weekend.

Senna and Hill did not run that afternoon, as a mark of respect, and at one stage I came across Georgie Hill sitting white and blank-faced on her husband's small motor scooter, almost in shock. She was lonely, vulnerable and shattered, a momentarily unwanted piece of human debris as the team continued its technical debriefing, an uncomplicated victim of the hard side of Formula One as she tried to come to terms with the death of a man she and Damon had liked, and to reassess the risk her husband and his ilk really faced. Nobody could possibly have guessed how much worse things would become the following day.

That sunny but cloudy afternoon Senna led off the line from his final pole position, but

Rude awakening. The 1994 Brazilian Grand Prix gave Hill an indication not only of Schumacher's challenge but how much work he faced trying to deal with Senna's speed.

for five laps the field circulated at slow speed behind the safety car after an accident on the startline involving J. J. Lehto and Pedro Lamy had spread debris everywhere. When the racing resumed Senna continued to lead for a lap, but on the seventh his Williams unaccountably failed to get through the 190+ mph Tamburello left-hander and struck the concrete outer wall at high speed. A stunned F1 fraternity was barely able to cope with the enormity of the news that the Brazilian had succumbed to his injuries, when it finally filtered through that evening. All through the paddock men and women alike wept.

The race had been stopped and restarted, surviving an accident in the pits in the closing stages, and resulting in another win for Schumacher. Damon Hill was sixth after a pit stop to repair a front wing damaged in an early brush with the German.

Behind the bald facts lies a story of bravery and cold-blooded commitment, for he went into the race uncertain just what had killed Senna, in a car identical to his own. Uncon-firmed reports suggest that the team disconnected the power-steering mechanism on his car – mainly because it was an unknown quantity rather than because it had been culpable – and as these words were written the official investigation into the cause of the accident had still to reach a definitive conclusion. Hill thus needed all his reserves of courage just to compete, let alone to race as hard as he did.

'Tragedy as it was with Ayrton, Damon did a terrific job in Imola,' said his mechanic Les Jones. 'He wasn't spooked about it on the grid. Obviously nobody knew what had caused the accident. When there's been a huge shunt like that it's always in the driver's mind, was there a failure, or whatever? It's got to be. But there was no sign of that at all. He was very calm and collected. It takes a lot to get him flustered or in a bad mood.

In the dreadful aftermath of Senna's accident at Imola, Hill drove heroically, even though at the time he had no firm knowledge of what had caused his team-mate's accident.

I HAD BREAKFAST WITH AYRTON. IN THE AFTERNOON HE WAS DEAD. IF HE HAD KNOWN WHAT WAS COMING, IT IS INCONCEIVABLE THAT HE WOULD HAVE STEPPED INTO HIS CAR.

'I don't think it's sunk in with many of us,' Les would say of Senna's death when we talked at the German Grand Prix in late July. 'It's been a strange season, because obviously some of us knew Roland and then with Ayrton dying; come the end of the season people will sit back and look at it a lot more than they are now. It's fortunate in a way that there wasn't much of a gap between Imola and Monaco and everybody got carried along, but it's the quiet moments where people look at it. I think it may sink in more for some when the pressure's off.'

Tellingly, Hill kept his own counsel, relying only on his family and close friends to help him through. 'Damon has never said anything

At Monaco a great start looked like making up for a nightmare in qualifying, until Hill and Hakkinen clashed at Ste Devote.

to me about it, but then that's Damon,' said Jones. 'He does keep a lot to himself.'

Hill's newspaper column, which appeared after each race, was traditionally penned by the writer Maurice Hamilton, but Damon insisted on writing the one after Imola himself. Without being maudlin or insincere, he provided a poignant insight into his relationship with Senna.

'I had breakfast with Ayrton,' he wrote. 'In the afternoon he was dead. If he had known what was coming, it is inconceivable that he would have stepped into his car. And yet on Sunday every driver knew that they could be killed by doing what they were doing. Roland had shown us all that death was ready and

waiting for the unfortunate, that we were all still vulnerable.

'Ayrton was no angel on the track and any views he had about safety were as much for his own self-preservation as for that of others. But he felt deeply shocked, as we all did, by Roland's crash and felt duty-bound to do something. Now he is dead, all those involved in the sport must think long and hard about what can be done to reduce the dangers and the correct ways to improve the show *without* compromising safety.'

If history had already repeated itself so many times as he emulated his father's climb to prominence, now it did so again. In 1968 Graham Hill had had the leadership of Team Lotus thrust upon him in the wake of Jim Clark's death. Now Damon Hill was forced to perform the same task.

Williams ran only one car at Monaco, where he qualified fourth after a struggle but was eliminated at the start after brushing with Hakkinen. The team had been all at sea throughout the meeting, and manager Ian Harrison was moved to comment: 'We were all victims of the general fall-out. To be honest, nobody wanted to be there. It was just one of those races to get through.' Schumacher won again.

In the Spanish Grand Prix Hill was joined by the man who had taken over his test role, the upcoming young Scot David Coulthard, and when Schumacher's Benetton mysteriously stuck in fifth gear Damon yet again emulated his father. Graham had brought Lotus back from the brink by winning the Spanish Grand Prix at Jarama; now Damon did the same for Williams at Barcelona. It was precisely the tonic that the demoralised team needed.

Nevertheless, behind the scenes there was unrest. In Canada Hill was a distant second again to Schumacher, and he and Coulthard had had a post-race spat after Damon criticised David's refusal to let him by once his own pursuit of the leaders had overtaxed his tyres. Now Renault Sport was pushing very hard for an established star to lead the team, and the name that was on their lips was Nigel Mansell's.

The critics had a field day. This, surely, proved that Hill had been rumbled, that his luck had finally run out. All the old arguments over Prost's level of commitment in 1993 were dragged out again. Undoubtedly he and Hill drove the best cars that season, so the critics based their reservations on one crucial fact. Had Prost been a true yardstick by which to

Like father, like son. Twenty-six years after Graham Hill had brought Lotus back, Hill's Spanish Grand Prix success lifted the shattered Williams team.

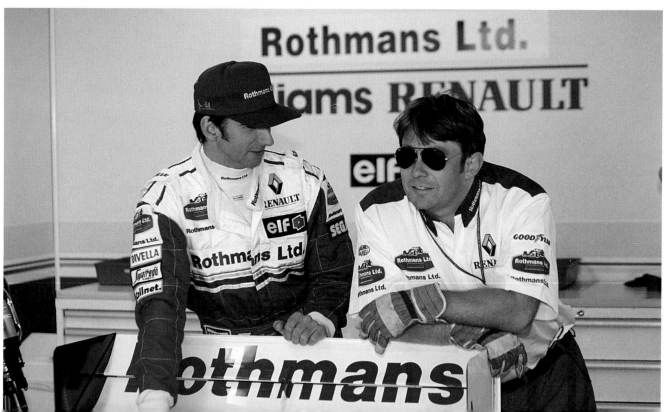

Racing is all about team-work. Hill, here with Les Jones, is liked and respected by his mechanics, and the feeling is reciprocated.

In Canada the Williams FW16 was no match for Schumacher's Benetton, but Hill salvaged second place prior to the post-race argument with team-mate Coulthard.

could there and everywhere else, just like everyone else.'

Nevertheless, the suspicion still lingered in some minds that Hill had had it easy against Prost. They pointed out how he always had to look at Prost's telemetry to learn where he was losing time. It's something that any driver will want to do when his team-mate is quicker. Often even when he isn't.

'The one thing that I think was very obvious last year was that Alain respected Damon for being a very good driver,' maintains Les Jones. 'Alain was so good on the throttle in mid-corner. His entry speed would be less than Damon's but Damon would brake harder and upset the balance of the car slightly, while Alain would be on the power earlier and be slightly quicker. But there wasn't a lot in it. It was body weight as much as anything.'

At the mandatory pre-season weigh-in at Kyalami, Hill had tipped the scales at seventy-three kilos, Prost at only sixty-three.

'The difference in the two body weights was the difference in the times, but saying that I think that Alain never went as quick as he could have gone. I think Magny-Cours was about as quick as he could go when Damon beat him to pole, the rest of the time, certainly in races, he only went as quick as he had to go.'

Did that mean that Hill was absolutely flat out but Prost wasn't?

'I don't know. It's such a difficult thing to say because Alain was such a precise driver and so intelligent. You listen to the radio, and he knew exactly what he had to do to win the race, and he was a very good tactician. Damon was very good on the radio, too. He's clear, he knows exactly what he wants to do. Very, very calm.

'A typical example is Magny-Cours in 1993 where there was a problem with the anti-lock brakes and the wheel speed sensors in prac-

'DAMON'S CLEAR, HE KNOWS EXACTLY WHAT HE WANTS TO DO. VERY, VERY CALM.'

judge others, or more of a metre rule? Was what you saw what you got, or was there more to Alain that wasn't always apparent? Was the calculating Frenchman merely drawing on just enough of his undoubted genius to beat his team-mate by a narrow margin, or was Hill really keeping him on his toes? Did the former champion have something in hand all the time?

Suggest any of that to Harrison, who has enormous respect for both drivers – and throw in the idea that Prost deliberately 'threw' the Belgian Grand Prix at Spa so that Hill might look better than he was, and thus be retained as his partner for 1994 instead of Senna – and the response was as swift as it was derisive. 'Bollocks! Alain was pushing as hard as he

As Schumacher celebrates his return to victory, Damon and Jean Alesi salute the crowd after finishing second and third respectively in Montreal.

A study in concentration. Hill is already in his own world as he prepares for the start in Canada.

tice. First lap out, obviously fired up but still calm and collected, he was half a second quicker than Alain.'

Some difference was to be expected, even if both drivers did possess similar levels of talent, for Prost was the veteran of well over a hundred races and had won fifty-one of them and three World Championships, while Hill was the newcomer whose Grand Prix score was just getting into double figures.

Damon was also becoming frustrated that Renault Sport did not appear to be placing as much store by his feedback as it had with Mansell, Prost and Senna, something that, in truth, was understandable given the outstanding information the latter pair in particular was renowned for providing. It must have put him in mind of his days with TOM'S in 1987, where hindsight indicated that his comments about the Toyota's initial lack of power were proved subsequently accurate.

The situation reached a head at Magny-Cours, where success in the French Grand Prix was vital to Renault, and for a rumoured fee of 1.5 million dollars Mansell was im-

ported for a guest appearance. Only eighteen months earlier managing director Patrick Faure had advised Frank Williams that if he ever employed Mansell again, it would mean saying goodbye to Renault. Now he was flavour of the month once more. Water flows very quickly under the F1 bridge.

In final qualifying Hill's mechanics accidentally installed two fifth gears, necessitating a lengthy delay during which Mansell set the fastest time. If ever Hill was going to lose control under pressure it was now. Instead, he drove brilliantly to beat the 1992 champion to pole position. 'It was a do-or-die issue,' confirmed Jones. 'I think he's underrated. A lot of people don't give him credit. Not the racing fraternity press, but the nationals give him a hard time and he's not given the credit that he deserves. He's very intelligent. His commitment within the team is incredible, I think. And since Ayrton's death . . .'

In the race Schumacher won yet again, after a scintillating start from the second row thrust him between the two Williams-Renaults. Hill fought brilliantly and outdrove Mansell, who

faded before retiring, but Benetton's cunning policy of stopping three times for fuel, to Williams's twice, would prove decisive. Nevertheless, Hill went to Silverstone convinced not only that he had made a point in France, but that he could win at home. Better still, he had scored a moral victory, for Mansell had firmly backed up his comments on the engine.

His British Grand Prix campaign got off to the worst possible start on Friday morning when the upper ends of the pushrods in the front suspension came undone, because their securing nuts had accidentally been left off.

'I wasn't even angry,' he admitted. 'Just in a state of disbelief. That sort of thing has never happened before, both sides doing that at once! I just watched it fold beneath me and I thought: What have I done?'

'I couldn't even articulate it over the radio. I was in total amazement. I parked the car and got a lift back to the pits, but then I saw Patrick Head walking in with his bags like he'd just got off the Number 29 bus from Clapham. I yelled at the guy to stop and leapt out, and there was Patrick confronted by his driver, and he'd barely even arrived for work. It wasn't a good start to his day . . . It really was the most bizarre thing I've ever seen!'

Most drivers would have administered a verbal beheading to the culprit, but Hill's reaction was calmer than most. 'But that goes into the way Damon feels about the team, the way he respects people that work on his car,' said Jones. 'He never ranted at anyone. Mechanics are human and everybody makes a mistake, and Damon's made mistakes where he's thrown it off the road, and we don't stand there and call him the biggest idiot alive. Among the crew he's well respected and well liked.'

Despite that setback he went on to win a thrilling shoot-out for pole position with Schumacher and Berger, his margin over

> 'MY HEART WAS IN MY MOUTH WATCHING MICHAEL GO ROUND, BUT NOT AS MUCH AS IT WAS IN MY MOUTH DOING MY LAP.'

Proving a point. In qualifying for the French Grand Prix Hill rose brilliantly to the challenge, despite mechanical problems, to snatch pole position.

The man who had motivated Hill to such effort was Nigel Mansell, the former champion who was wooed back into the fold by Renault Sport's desperation for a home victory.

the German three thousandths of a second.

'You have to be determined to want it enough and today I was determined to want it more than the other guys. My heart was in my mouth watching Michael go round, but not as much as it was in my mouth doing my lap.

'It was just simply a case of now or never. You know you cannot come away from a lap like that – and your last shot at getting pole position – and wish later you had gone a bit quicker somewhere.'

The following day he barely put a wheel wrong as he stormed to the victory that had so eluded his father. Almost paranoid after Schumacher had beaten him off the line in France, he was determined to make the most of his pole position this time, and led the field into Copse corner. 'I was actually craning my neck to see him,' he said of Schumacher. 'I thought he must be alongside in my blind

spot.' This time, however, the German was some metres back, and until the first fuel stops Damon controlled the race. He came into the pits marginally slower; however, and when both had refuelled it was Schumacher in the lead and a fierce battle was in prospect, for Hill was in no mood to be denied.

The two of them were still only seconds apart when Schumacher finally obeyed the black flag, which had been hung out to him for five laps. This is the universal and immutable signal that a driver must come into the pits, and he is supposed to obey immediately. During the warm-up laps prior to the start, when the grid is formed, Schumacher had illegally overtaken Hill, and had now been given a five second stop-and-go penalty, but his team had ordered him to stay out while it tried to argue to have the black flag and the penalty withdrawn. Eventually he complied and Hill went on to his great triumph. For Schumacher, the infringement would have dramatic consequences.

Nothing could mar Hill's day. 'I feel superb,' he smiled, a man totally at peace with himself. 'This is the best day of my life. It's like a dream, and I want to thank everybody at Williams who has been through the misery of this year. It's been a tough one, and I want to thank everyone for getting behind me.

'Immediately afterwards my Mum was choked. My sisters were the same, unable to speak. Georgie kept smiling and kissing me. Even grown men kept wanting to give me a hug – which was a bit worrying!

'But it was perfectly understandable. After all these years, to have the name Hill engraved on the British Grand Prix trophy is a wonderful, wonderful feeling.

Later, relaxing in the paddock, he drew on all his experience from the adolescent punk band for whom he had played bass guitar – rather colourfully named Sex Hitler and the Hormones – to join Eddie Irvine, Johnny Herbert and Eddie Jordan on stage at the latter's post-race paddock bash.

'He's doing a good job, you can't take it away from the bloke,' said Harrison later, referring to his driving if not his musical ability. 'If I were in his boots and everybody was saying how Nigel Mansell has spurred the team on, I'd be hacked off. Especially as Damon was on pole in France and again in Britain.

'I'm surprised he found that much. I think he's gone up another gear. He always gives one hundred per cent, and we have improved the car a bit, but perhaps he's just more confident. If he can sustain this, he can aspire to a new level. At Silverstone he really wrung the car's neck. I don't think anyone could have gone quicker.' Not even Mansell, was the inference from many others who echoed such sentiments.

Neither, secretly, did Hill. He had proved another point. Over winter there had been suggestions, following a couple of testing incidents, that he was struggling in an F1 car fitted with standard 'passive' suspension in place of the now outlawed computer-controlled 'active'

system, which he had been instrumental in developing. Jones was sceptical. 'I don't think so. He did a great majority of the development on active and traction control, but over the winter he adapted without it and when we got to the first race the difference in the times was Damon and Ayrton.

'Overall he's driven good races. The car wasn't the best car we'd ever produced, but he proved when Nigel came that he's doing a very good job with the equipment, and to pull those laps out in France and Britain.'

Mansell might not have sat in an F1 car since Adelaide in November 1992, but it wasn't as if he was out of condition for racing,

Just good friends. Coulthard and Hill had an uneasy alliance, the newcomer anxious to make his mark, the latter focussing everything on his championship challenge.

having competed ever since in the IndyCar championship. All he really lacked in France had been the sheer stamina, something only racing F1 cars specifically could bring back fully. Qualifying showed he'd lost little, if anything, of his basic speed. To his credit, he'd been one of the first to congratulate Damon.

Germany two weeks later brought Hill down to earth in an uncomfortable landing, for this was where the Ferraris were resurgent in qualifying, and where Gerhard Berger won a race that saw eleven cars damaged or eliminated on the first lap. It could have been a cakewalk for Williams, but one of these was Hill's, who collided with Ukyo Katayama's Tyrrell while challenging for third place.

It would have been all too easy for him to fall back on the line many other 'stars' would have been tempted to adopt, and to have blamed Katayama, for the Japanese driver was new to the front end of the grid and the race, and was an easy target. Instead, Hill was ruthlessly honest with himself and his public.

'I missed a golden opportunity today,' he admitted. 'I touched Katayama trying to pass him at the third chicane. Perhaps if I had been more patient then I could have won this race. What I did is try to pass and then thought it wasn't going to work, and then I tried to pull out of it. I had seen him make room for Michael and I thought he was going to do the same for me. I guess it's one of those things when you have someone you are not used to racing against you don't know what they are going to do. At the time I didn't know how competitive Michael and Gerhard were going to be – if I knew then what I know now I would have sat back.'

He was classified eighth, and what made the wound worse was that Katayama only lasted

After the disappointment of 1993, triumph at the British Grand Prix finally brought the Hill family the victory so often denied Graham. It was indeed an emotional day.

After Magny-Cours, Hill was paranoid about Schumacher's starts, but at Silverstone he had a clear upper hand in the British Grand Prix.

Hill poses with fellow countrymen Eddie Irvine, Mark Blundell, Martin Brundle and Johnny Herbert, all of whom entertained private thoughts about his own success.

until the seventh lap before retiring, while for once Schumacher too went on the list after dropping out with electrical trouble after twenty-one.

Schumacher should not really have been racing, for after his Silverstone incident he had been given a two-race suspension which should have started in Germany. However, mindful of the intensity of his fans' enthusiasm, the sport's governing body, the Federation Internationale Automobile allowed him to race pending an appeal to be heard late in August, just after the Belgian Grand Prix.

There was more bad news for him, too, just before the meeting got underway, when the FIA let it be known that its investigation into the onboard computer software used by Benetton in the San Marino Grand Prix – which Benetton had only just allowed it to examine – revealed a facility for an illegal automatic start 'launch control' system which acted as a driver aid to help him get off the line faster. The FIA made it clear that the available evidence suggested that the programme, though well concealed, had not been used, and Benetton claimed that it was a redundant part of a complex system that had simply not been deleted, but some of the mud

had begun to stick and questions were being asked about the legitimacy of Benetton's performances.

Though this appeared to load the dice a little more firmly in his favour, especially since Schumacher's six points from Silverstone had been taken away, Hill himself could not afford to relax during the weekend after becoming the target of death threats.

'Motor racing is dangerous enough at the best of times,' he said, 'but on Sunday I had to get through with the added complication of a death threat if I showed any signs of beating Michael.

'The call came through to the Rothmans Williams-Renault team on Friday, the message being that if I was ahead of him, then I would be shot on Sunday. Since my main purpose was to beat him, I was not prepared to accept the obvious get-out option.'

It was almost certainly a crank, but he took the precaution of using a back entrance to the circuit each day and having a police escort. 'There was even someone on duty outside my bedroom door each night.

'Under circumstances such as that, it is difficult to feel relaxed! Certainly, I couldn't enjoy quite so much the banter with the German race fans, most of whom were fantastic; very friendly. But I must admit, there was an undercurrent of animosity whipped up by the media reports on Schumacher's two-race ban.'

Nothing came of the threats, but altogether it was an unsettling weekend, especially with the crowd's firecrackers which kept exploding all the way through and sounded like gunshots. Hungary, three weeks later, would also be unsettling. Schumacher was still competing, and he dominated qualifying and the race, Benetton again utilising the three-stop

At Hockenheim victory was there for the taking, until Hill collided with Katayama. Eighth place was a crushing disappointment, but at least he was honest about his error.

refuelling policy that had been superior to Williams's two in Magny-Cours, with similar results. Damon was second, but a long way behind, and his problems getting through lapped traffic on this tight course did not sit well with some team members who could never have envisaged Senna making such a meal of it.

The odds now seemed even more firmly tilted in Schumacher's favour, with the German on seventy-six points to Hill's forty-five, but other factors were at work behind the scenes.

Schumacher still had to miss two races, unless his appeal was upheld after Spa, but the Belgian race was to become another crucial turning point in a series of misfortunes.

AS HIS CHAMPIONSHIP CHALLENGE COINCIDED WITH THE EXTRA PRESSURE, CRACKS BEGAN TO SHOW IN HIS EQUANIMITY.

Hill went to the majestic track confident not only that it would suit his Williams-Renault perfectly, but that modifications to the once daunting Eau Rouge corner would actually work against the Benetton. The weather in qualifying was soaking, however, which made the race a lottery, and when conditions dried out everyone was forced to estimate their chassis settings.

Schumacher quickly took the lead from the Brazilian driver Rubens Barrichello, who had won pole position with a bit of neat judgement as the track was drying out right to the last minute, but it was some time before Hill was finally able to push into second place. The man preventing him from moving up was Coulthard, who had gone by when they both stopped for fuel.

Hill waited for the team to order the Scot to move over, then radioed to the pits when he didn't. 'I let them know my feelings and they replied, "Yes, we understand what you are saying." But nothing happened. Once I got past him I was running much quicker because I was not in dirty air.'

Qualifying at Spa was a lottery, as the track started out wet and only just became dry enough to risk slick tyres at the end. Hill was third fastest.

It was the first real sign of another shifting balance within Williams, and it was to be a while before possible reasons began to emerge. Williams was increasingly having to weigh up the best solution to the three-into-two scenario it was likely to face in 1995 when either Michael Schumacher or Nigel Mansell might have one of its seats, something that would necessitate a choice between Hill and Coulthard as the second driver. Hill was all too well aware of this, and as his championship challenge coincided with this extra pressure, cracks began to show in his equanimity.

Before the start Coulthard had quietly ad-

vised him to be aware that Barrichello, on pole just ahead of him, was not always the quickest starter when the two had raced together in F3000. He reminded him just before the off, only to have Damon fly into an uncharacteristic rage, as if he felt the Scot was simply trying to outpsych him. The outburst created a bad atmosphere within the team, which perhaps explained its reluctance to instruct Coulthard to relinquish his second place. At the same time, it was seen within F1 circles as a crass waste of Hill's chances of catching Schumacher.

The German duly won by 13.6 seconds, but he immediately ran into yet further contro-

versy when the strip of wood beneath his car – the so-called 'plank' that had been made mandatory on all cars to reduce their aerodynamic downforce and grip from Hockenheim onwards – did not conform to the regulations and may have conferred an unfair performance advantage. Hill, after all, was the winner. It was the start of a bad week for Schumacher.

His appeal against exclusion from the Italian and Portuguese Grands Prix, following the Silverstone black flag controversy, was rejected two days later, and the following week his appeal against exclusion from the Belgian race also failed. On that occasion Benetton was let off for an infringement of the refuelling regulations in Germany, which had come to light after its car driven by Jos Verstappen had caught fire following a fuel leak. Though that alleviated the immediate fear that the team might be thrown out of the championship, it did little to assuage Schumacher's increasing anger. There were stories circulating again that he was continuing his talks with Williams, as well as with McLaren.

All this should have been good news for Damon Hill as he headed for Monza and an Italian Grand Prix that he simply had to win. Far from removing the pressure on Damon, Schumacher's absence simply increased it. Now victory was expected of him.

There were further factors at work, when Damon turned up in Monza with his lawyer and accountant as well as the ever-supportive Georgie, desperately hoping to push Frank Williams towards a decision about the option he had on his services for 1995. This was due to expire on 15 September, and Hill was anxious to have matters sorted out as quickly as possible. With the Schumacher/Mansell situation far from being settled, however, Williams was in no mood to play ball.

Within the team the atmosphere had curdled even more as the pressure mounted, for Hill had now asked that his race engineer John Russell be replaced with the highly experienced David Brown, who had masterminded car set-up for Mansell, Prost and Senna. It was a crushing blow for the outspoken but extremely loyal Russell, and created further difficulties. Insiders hinted at broken relationships and acrimony. The tension, on and off the track, was mounting.

There was more bad news when the two Ferraris of Jean Alesi and Gerhard Berger were the fastest in qualifying, and a nasty

'THERE DOESN'T SEEM TO BE ANY LET-UP IN THIS GAME, AND IT DOESN'T MATTER WHO YOU HAVE AS YOUR TEAM-MATE BECAUSE EVERYONE IN F1 IS QUICK.'

When Hill sprayed the champagne at the Belgian GP, inwardly he was raging after finishing only second. The 'win' would be awarded later.

shock at one stage when old F3 rival Johnny Herbert suddenly vaulted back on to form with a new Mugen-Honda V10 engine, which transformed his Lotus and all but made it a match for the Williams. At the start of the race, the Lotus was up to third when they funnelled behind the Ferraris into the tight first chicane. Hill had already conceded the place, anxious not to get embroiled in any shoving and clearly mindful of his tangle there with Senna the previous year.

'Damon was very edgy at the drivers' briefing,' Herbert remembered. 'I accidentally touched his foot at one stage, and he jumped a mile!'

Perhaps the caution paid, though, for Herbert was pushed into a spin when Eddie Irvine tried a rash late-braking move round the outside of his Williams. The race was temporarily stopped, and when it resumed Hill challenged Berger for second place in Alesi's

wake. The Frenchman's gearbox broke after fifteen laps, then Berger's short lead was lost when he was baulked in the pits. But when Damon stopped for fuel, Coulthard's own stop was quicker and the Scot took over the lead. This time, however, there was no question that Williams had to favour Hill, and on the twenty-ninth lap David pointedly slowed on the straight past the pits to let Damon retake the lead. After that the two of them drove round nose-to-tail until the final lap. As Hill cruised to his seventh Grand Prix triumph, Coulthard ran out of fuel in the last corner.

Damon's relief was obvious afterwards. 'I feel this was a well-deserved victory by the Rothmans-Williams-Renault team, and I would have loved to have David up there with me as he played a big part in this weekend and deserved to be on the podium,' he said.

This was more the normal Hill speaking, but earlier he had given an insight into the pressures of modern-day F1 as he talked about team-mates.

'There doesn't seem to be any let-up in this game and it doesn't matter who you have as your team-mate because everyone in F1 is quick. If it was any other way it wouldn't be the same challenge.

'The competition with your team-mate is part of the excitement. There are other teams out there, of course, but they have different equipment. In our team David is very quickly coming to grips with the technique, and he is pushing me. It is by having competition inside the team that we are both able to go forward. The team-mates that I have had have all been rather high calibre, and Nigel is certainly another in that class. He is going to be dynamite when he

A lucky escape. Minutes after the start of the Italian GP, Berger chases Alesi out of the picture, as Irvine (15) nudges Herbert (12) into his spin. Hill was just able to avoid hitting the front of the Lotus.

comes back to Formula One; that's the way he drives.'

Now, as he headed to the Portuguese Grand Prix at Estoril, Hill had his sights set on another ten points, to narrow the deficit to one. 'We must be on a par with Schumacher when he gets back,' he said.

He duly won again in Portugal, confirming Schumacher's worst expectations, but when the German returned in time for the European GP at Jerez, he was able to turn the tables, beating Hill in a tactical race that saw Mansell once again return to the Williams camp. Now the controversial 1994 World Championship moved inexorably towards its climax, with only the Japanese and Australian Grands Prix remaining. If Schumacher beat Hill in Japan he was champion, but in the Orient, Hill drove his greatest race to prolong the contest, beating Schumacher fair and square in appalling weather.

'I drove on a completely different level that day,' he recalled with a dark smile of complete satisfaction. 'I was in what I call a twilight zone of driving, where I just offered myself up completely to my instincts. It was

Hill's second consecutive victory at Monza was a massive relief from the pressure that had been mounting all weekend and took him to within eleven points of Schumacher.

Over and out: Schumacher's Benetton teeters on two wheels, almost obscuring Hill's Williams, following the controversial manoeuvre in Adelaide, which clinched the German's first World Championship.

fantastic. The satisfaction of that victory was tremendous.'

Torrential rain beset the event, causing stoppage and a restart, and several drivers to crash when their low-slung cars simply aquaplaned off the road on puddles of standing water. Hill's task was made even more difficult and dangerous when his right rear wheel could not be changed during his solitary pit stop because the wheel nut jammed. He thus had to resume his lead with three new tyres and a worn one, and as the team kept this news from him, he grappled with the han-

dling imbalance and a growing challenge from Schumacher. Going into the nail-biting last lap the German was just over two seconds behind and gaining, but Hill opened the gap again to cross the line first after a brilliant display that kept his World Championship dreams alive. Going down to Adelaide, he and Schumacher were now just a point apart, and the stage was set for the final confrontation, *mano a mano*.

Back in the swing of F1 again, Mansell rose to the occasion Down Under to put both young contenders in their place as he took

a shade under three seconds behind the Benetton when Schumacher made a remarkable unenforced error on the thirty-sixth lap, clouting a concrete wall very hard with his right-hand suspension after sliding right across the grass. As Hill arrived on the scene, Schumacher was limping on the left-hand side of the track. Seeing a gap to the right, and subconsciously realising that the Benetton was going slowly, Hill pounced. Seeing his move, Schumacher veered right, across his bows, and the two cars collided as they reached the corner. The Benetton teetered on to its left-hand wheels, almost flipping over, before landing heavily and spearing out of the race on the left-hand side of the road. Hill carried on, with his fans back in England watching ecstatically at the thought that all he now had to do was finish fifth to beat Schumacher by a point. But then the speed of the Williams foretold fresh drama. Its left front tyre was deflated.

Hill limped back to the pits, where the full truth emerged. The left front suspension's pullrod was broken, and repair would have taken too long. He, too, was out of the race, and out on the circuit Schumacher punched the air in delight as the news filtered through that his brutal tactics had, after all, won him the world crown.

If Damon Hill shared the view of many observers that it was tarnished by Schumacher's extraordinary and deliberate swerve, he kept his own dignified counsel, refusing to lower himself to mud-slinging. 'If I had known that Michael had just hit the wall I might not have tried to pass him so soon,' he said later. 'But hindsight is a wonderful thing. I'm a racing driver; I didn't know that Michael had gone off, I came round the corner, saw him where I would hardly have expected him to be, and saw a gap that was big enough at that time. In those circumstances I'd do the same thing again.'

In the end he had lost, as controversially as Alain Prost had lost to Ayrton Senna in the fight for the 1990 championship, but he would be back. The manner of his defeat merely strengthened his resolve.

pole position in qualifying. Then Hill's cause was helped when Schumacher crashed heavily in his intended race car, while trying to beat Mansell's time. He was unharmed, but the incident betrayed the unexpected vulnerability that he was to display on race day.

Schumacher and Hill made short work of Mansell at the start, sprinting ahead before the first corner to begin a gripping duel that rarely saw them more than a second apart until Hill lost time lapping Heinz-Harald Frentzen (who would replace him at Williams for 1997). Hill had thus dropped to

6

HAMMERED IN THE CRUCIBLE

'OBVIOUSLY I AM SEEKING TO WIN THE
WORLD CHAMPIONSHIP. I HAVE THE RIGHT
PACKAGE AND I'VE GOT THE EXPERIENCE.
THERE'S EVERY GOOD REASON TO
BELIEVE THAT I CAN DO IT.'

Damon Hill began 1995 full of confidence, itching to get his hands on Williams's new FW17 chassis with its Benetton-like high nose and revised three-litre Renault engine. 'I believe in myself that I have the arsenal to attack the championship. This is going to be one of the tightest years for a long time; there's so many people in it. But in some ways that can be good.'

After the first three races it looked as if his aspirations were going to be realised, but after another bruising and acrimonious battle, Michael Schumacher again beat him to the title, and the tabloid newspapers in England tore him apart. It was a brutal year for the quiet and deeply introspective Englishman, as he revealed in a detailed conversation in Suzuka. That, too, would be another disastrous race for him when he spun off on the forty-first lap while running well behind Schumacher, but it also revealed the depth of his resilience. Mentally, he was shaking off the disappointment of 1995, and raising his sights to 1996. In F1, hope springs eternal.

The hardest part of it all had been the continual criticism, much of it unjustified. He shrugged. 'I didn't win the championship. If I'd won it, they'd love me.' This was true, but it still hurt.

'It's difficult when you set yourself a goal of trying to succeed in a sport,' he said. 'When you get to a certain level you think by virtue of what you've achieved and the level at which you are performing, that you should intrinsically inspire a certain amount of respect. But they are very demanding. I represent my country in sport, and the press are hungry for stories of success. If you don't provide success they look for a reason. I can't deny it; it upsets me a lot. And it doesn't make my job any easier, because the criticism can be quite destructive . . .'

Hill has always been a victim of his benign nature. Where a driver such as Nigel Mansell would brook no criticism and would exact petty revenge on miscreants, Hill lets the situation ride. 'I wouldn't say I'm easy going, but

> 'I DIDN'T WIN THE WORLD CHAMPIONSHIP. IF I'D WON IT, THEY'D LOVE ME. I REPRESENT MY COUNTRY IN SPORT, AND THE PRESS ARE HUNGRY FOR STORIES OF SUCCESS.'

The angle of Hill's right front wheel tells its own story in the Senna corner at Interlagos, as suspension failure deprives him of victory in the 1995 Brazilian GP.

I like to have a good relationship. I don't like confrontation. Maybe I should shun some people, because at the end of the day journalists need stories and I can either help them on that score or not. But that's not part of my character. Maybe it should be . . .'

Part of the criticism centred, inevitably, on his clashes with Schumacher which had marred his 1995 campaign and which had allowed the German to accuse him of trying to even the score for Adelaide 1994. But had force of circumstance dragged him into negative situations, or were they simply inevitable given the pressures in modern 'sport'? 'My lesson from this year is that I got drawn into trying to recover for the lost momentum which we suffered in the early part of the season through mechanical problems. Instead of perhaps biding my time and staying in the fight, I went for the victory at all costs. And it was very costly! That's something which is not really my philosophy, so not being true to yourself and not sticking to what you know to be the right way of doing things was a bit of an error,' he explained. Being true to yourself is a key expression in Hill's vocabulary, indicating a character in which self-esteem surpasses many other emotions.

'The times I have performed best are the times when I have done things my way,' he added, but a laugh robbed the statement of arrogance.

Hill is a throwback to Raymond Sommer, a great French privateer racer of the 1930s and 1940s, to whom the style in which you fought was at least as important as the result you achieved. 'It's not as satisfying to win by default,' Hill insisted. 'It's got to be honourable. See, what sport should be about, and is about for me, is proving things to myself. I start with the premise of "I don't know what I'm capable of doing, and I'm going to enter into a competitive environment to see what I am capable of doing." And I've found out more about myself doing this sport than I would ever believe possible. Some of the things I do, I come away feeling so incredibly proud of myself. That element is very important to me.

'If I drove absolutely brilliantly and I fin-ished third and got a lot of criticism for it, that wouldn't bother me because I would know myself that I'd brought my performance to a level I considered the best I could do. You can only do your best. You can improve, but at a given time you can only do your best. If I felt I hadn't done my best I would hate myself, would tend to listen to criticism too much, and then life becomes very uncomfortable. There are times this year when I have

not been happy with my performance and have come in for a lot of criticism, and it's knocked the stuffing out of me.'

It had been a transitional year, trying to hone a harder edge against his better nature. And it had begun well as he dominated the Brazilian GP until his suspension failed. He then took victories in Argentina and Imola, the latter an emotional catharsis for F1 in general and Williams in particular after the sad events of the previous season. The Spanish GP at Barcelona was the fourth race of the series, and it was there that Schumacher and Benetton gave rude notice that, despite its knife-edge handling, their B196 chassis, which now enjoyed the same Renault power as Hill's Williams, was a definite contender. Schumacher won, with teammate Johnny Herbert second, and Hill dropped out of the runner-up slot in sight of the flag when his Williams slumped to fourth with a problem with the engine-driven hydraulic pump.

As Hill railed at Williams, Frank reminded

In Argentina, the Williams ran like clockwork, giving Hill a comfortable win.

Yet again, the first corner at Monaco brought carnage, after Coulthard and the Ferraris collided. Hill took the restart, but was soundly drubbed by Schumacher.

him coldly: 'Williams is a team that wins together, and loses together.'

In Monaco Hill earned pole position after a brilliant and gripping fight with Schumacher, but come the race, Benetton had superior strategy and the German was again in demoralisingly good form. Hill was a beaten second.

'We returned to Barcelona for testing in the week after the GP and we also found improvements in the set-up of the car which enabled us to go 1.4 seconds quicker than we went in qualifying,' he said. To some observers his fortitude was beginning to smack of whistling to keep his spirits up.

Hill could have won in Canada, where Schumacher for once had an electrical problem that dropped him to an eventual fifth place, but this was Jean Alesi's day in the Ferrari. The Williams again suffered hydraulic pump failure, and he coasted to a halt along the pit wall before vaulting out for another verbal spat with Frank. Pole position did little to improve things in France, for Schumacher was yet again dominant in the race as he took victory again by more than half a minute. Hill was now trailing him by eleven points, and the early promise of a championship triumph appeared to have evaporated along with the spirit of goodwill within the Williams camp. Patrick Head was again reminded how much quicker Mansell had been than Hill through the fast corners at Suzuka in qualifying the

previous year, and more than one voice within the team wondered aloud how much Hill was losing out to Schumacher on entry and exit to and from the pits during refuelling stops, too.

What Williams could not fathom at this stage was how an early race advantage could so firmly be reversed by Schumacher and Benetton, and to add to their demoralisation, their rivals turned on another devastating display at Silverstone during the British GP.

At this stage of the season the popular view was that the Williams was far and away the best car, which put its drivers under even more pressure to excel in it. 'It's an adaptable car,' Hill confirmed. 'We can usually find a good balance, but now it seems that we are starting to lose out in the performance stakes. I think we are aware that there's some work to be done.'

But still the world saw it as the best, and expected results. On home ground, Hill took pole position, and as Alesi held up Schumacher, he romped into a healthy lead. Schumacher took over when Hill made his first refuelling stop, and it became agonisingly clear to Williams that they had been

'THERE ARE TIMES THIS YEAR WHEN I HAVE NOT BEEN HAPPY WITH MY PERFORMANCE AND HAVE COME IN FOR A LOT OF CRITICISM, AND IT'S KNOCKED THE STUFFING OUT OF ME.'

Hill does the business with the champagne as he and Williams celebrate an emotional triumph at Imola, which stretched his World Championship lead and helped ease the memories of the 1994 tragedy.

Winding down: at Silverstone, Hill put his controversial clash with Schumacher behind him when he stepped on stage to strum bass guitar.

duped again. Where Hill was scheduled to stop twice, Schumacher was going to make do with only one. Suddenly, the complexion of the race had changed completely.

Schumacher's stop on lap thirty-one lasted just over thirteen seconds, and with a series of fastest laps Hill tried to build the advantage he needed for his second pit stop. But it was not enough. When he rejoined the race on the forty-first lap, Schumacher went ahead again.

On the forty-sixth lap, Hill thought he saw a chance as they came through the quick right-hand corner called Bridge, which leads to the braking area for the tight left-hander, Priory. He was some way behind the Benetton, and when he tried to outbrake it, the two of them collided and ended their race in the gravel bed. It was, in truth, a remarkably clumsy effort by Hill, and the national tabloid dailies tore into him to such an extent that Herbert's first triumph went largely unnoticed. The papers also made much of alleged critical remarks against Hill by Frank Williams himself, who had never made any secret of his desire to sign Schumacher one day.

Even Hill's explanation sounded feeble. 'I thought I saw an opportunity that I could take advantage of. But I'm afraid Michael is a harder man to pass than that.'

Schumacher, the innocent party on this occasion, fired some more shots in their psychological war, claiming with outrageous front that it was what Hill had done in Adelaide.

Just as it seemed that things could not possibly get worse, Hill threw away the satisfaction of stealing pole position from Schumacher at Hockenheim, right in front of the champion's rampantly chauvinistic fans, by spinning at the first corner just as he had opened a huge lead on the first lap. There was speculation that a faulty wheel bearing might have helped him off the road, but by now a dye was cast and the tabloids mauled him all over again. Schumacher won again, and was now nineteen points ahead.

In Hungary Hill was finally able to fight back, taking a decisive victory and even showing Schumacher a wheel on the one occasion that the German got close enough to challenge him for the lead. Hill would later describe his success as the best race of his life, and seeing the Benetton expire in the closing stages must have made it seem even sweeter. That weekend, he and his manager Michael Breen had also concluded a lucrative deal with Williams for 1996, and it seemed as if a corner had finally been turned. But that was before Spa, and yet another psychologically punishing defeat after a wheel-to-wheel battle with Schumacher.

The two of them were now separated by only eleven points. 'I feel a lot happier after Hungary,' Hill admitted during qualifying at Spa-Francorchamps for the Belgian GP. 'But it's worthwhile pointing out that there is still some way to go before I am leading the championship. But yes, I am still a damn sight better off after Hungary.' He had celebrated afterwards, he admitted, 'But not for too long. I was down in the dumps after Silverstone and Hockenheim, but since then we've rebounded quite well. I knew if I lost in Hungary that I could virtually discount winning the championship. Michael is odds-on favourite, but I am feeling good about the prospects at present. We have got a competitive package and things are going in the right direction. We have the sort of momentum back that we had at Imola, but our advantage is closer now over Benetton and Ferrari than it was then. I would never underestimate Benetton. But we can push forward again. I believe that it is going to be very tight now in qualifying and races until the end of the year.'

He was asked whether he would put money on himself to win the championship, and he smiled tolerantly. 'Well, I have got money on it . . . I've invested my entire career on it! Last year was close, and this year the championship is certainly my goal.'

What did he think Michael was feeling? Who had more pressure on him? 'Well, I have a lot of inner pressure from myself to perform, but most drivers have that. But perhaps there is more pressure on Michael because he has the possibility to lose the title which, only a fortnight ago, was beginning to look quite secure. He could be feeling more twitchy.'

Two days later, however, he was the one feeling uncomfortable. In changeable conditions on a track suddenly dampened by rain, Hill seemed to be set for victory after changing tyres at just the right moment. Schumacher was still on slick tyres as Hill sped on to his tail, but then the rain stopped, and with some ruthless blocking tactics the champion was able to keep his adversary at bay until a dry line appeared again and he was able to pull away to victory. Without question, Schumacher's car control was brilliant in the conditions, but views on the acceptability of his methods for keeping Hill behind varied according to sense of sportsmanship and the length and depth of one's interest in motorsport. To the anything goes 'modernists', Schumacher had controlled things superbly, and Hill was little more than a wimp. The reality was rather more complicated than that.

'This is supposed to be a sport, isn't it?' Hill snapped. 'It seems that Michael is happy to use any means of preventing anybody else winning. I'm just not prepared to resort to similar tactics.' And he sought clarification from the governing body as to what tactics it was prepared to accept from drivers.

'I think Michael is prepared to do anything necessary to win, it seems, including not letting the other person past. He's a hard customer. It's really a matter of pursuing your own line of ethics, where you draw the line,

what tactics you employ. Each to his own.

'I find it difficult to have a relationship with him, because we are completely different characters. We see each other at races, of course, but apart from saying "Hello" or "Good Morning", there's little that we have to say to one another. I find him cold and aloof. We are just two totally different personalities, that's just the way that it is. There's nothing either of us can do about that. You just have to accept it.

'Having said that, I don't honestly think it's possible for anybody at the top of the sport, fighting for the World Championship, to get on terribly easily. Things are bound to be a little bit strained. I think motor racing is very much like boxing. You end up with two people out there, focusing on trying to beat each other. It's usually your team-mate; that's the

The tale of woe continued at Hockenheim where, having stolen pole position from local hero Schumacher, Hill spun away a healthy lead at the start of the second lap.

normal situation because your team-mate is always the first man you've got to beat. But whoever it is, you do tend to find that the competitive urge makes it necessary to feel some sort of degree of aggression to the other person. But the idea is to control that and to channel it positively, to make yourself perform better. That's what sport is for, isn't it? It's an alternative for aggression.

'Some people suggest that these days sport really should be like a boxing match, pushing and shoving and no regard for the rules, but I don't care for that. I can do that; I could weave all over the track, I could knock the other guy off. I could do that, but it's not in the rules. The rules are that you don't do it. If I did it, I'd get a suspended race ban, or I'd get an immediate ban.'

As it transpired, the timing of these words was a trifle unfortunate, for at the next race, at Monza, Hill and Schumacher had another controversial collision . . .

Schumacher's tactics at Spa were the sort you can find in many undisciplined leisure karting operations. 'And you know what happens then?' Hill said sharply. 'They go over the top of each other and break each other's necks . . . That's what happens.'

He would not be drawn into discussion about Schumacher in comparison with Senna, even though he had raced wheel-to-wheel with both. 'I don't really want to talk about that, it's not for me to say. Ayrton wasn't a saint, was he? He was in the business to win, and he was pretty ruthless.

'The spirit of the thing has suffered. The times have changed and the ethics have changed. You just have to make your own choice, don't you? And then live with it. Michael obviously has, and so have I. He is obviously an extremely talented driver, and you have to respect his ability. He is, of course, a great competitor and you can never take away from his speed and aggression.'

The incident at Monza was triggered as Schumacher and Hill, fighting for the lead as expected, came up to lap the Japanese rookie Taki Inoue. Schumacher scythed by Inoue's Arrows approaching the second chicane, but Hill was momentarily distracted as Inoue changed his line. Initially the Japanese driver moved back on to the race line after letting Schumacher by, then belatedly moved for Hill when he suddenly saw him. By then, Hill was preparing to make other arrangements, and in the confusion he missed his braking point and ran into the back of Schumacher's Benetton, shoving both cars into inglorious

retirement in the gravel bed. This time the innocent Schumacher waved an angry and admonishing finger at him before stalking off. Hill was mortified. 'Obviously Michael is very upset, but I'm upset too,' he said. 'I would never have wanted to tangle deliberately.'

His season was rapidly falling apart. In Portugal, Coulthard won his first Grand Prix, while three-stop Schumacher caught and passed two-stop Hill.

In Estoril, Frank Williams was philosophical about Hill's much publicised accidents. 'Most accidents are accidents,' he said. 'Something happens, not by design or because it was done deliberately. People are human beings, and humans make the occasional mistake. That cannot be prevented. I cannot give you my opinion on whether or not the press spends too much time analysing accidents. But I recognise that they have to write something. And if the accidents are important to them, then clearly it is good value to them insofar as it helps to sell newspapers. I understand that.'

And he was asked for his views on the respective qualities of the two rivals. 'The most important thing for you guys is that they always have accidents and help you fill your newspapers!' Frank replied, tongue-in-cheek. 'Apart from that, one of the guys has won a championship and the other has not.' And though Frank didn't say it, the 'other' did not look likely to redress that imbalance as the season progressed.

Besides the obvious disappointment of losing the championship to Schumacher, Hill later revealed that the European Grand Prix, which followed at Germany's Nürburgring circuit, was his single biggest regret of the season. Almost lost in the indignity of an erratic exit as he tried to make up time after losing the lead – and his nose wing – in a clash with Jean Alesi in the Ferrari, was the fact that he

> 'SOME PEOPLE SUGGEST THAT THESE DAYS SPORT SHOULD BE A BOXING MATCH, PUSHING AND SHOVING AND NO REGARD FOR THE RULES, BUT I DON'T CARE FOR THAT.'

had overtaken Schumacher in a spell of dramatic side-by-side motoring in which he slogged it out wheel-to-wheel with the German, only to throw it all away very shortly afterwards with a minor error in the last corner, which allowed the Benetton driver to skip past again. By now observers were seeking the negative points, not the positive.

'I don't think I ever felt so down as I did after the Nürburgring,' he confessed. 'I knew I could have won that race. And I was quicker than anyone on the track. As it turned out I had only one more stop to make than Michael, so I was one stop up on him, ahead of him on the track, and I underestimated how aggressively Alesi was going to defend his position. So it was a very sad race for me. I don't think there was anything wrong with my driving at all, it's just that I made the wrong assumption about Jean!'

It was another ignominious retirement that all but confirmed the German's second championship, and though he didn't realise it at the time, Hill had sustained a fractured leg. 'It's a hairline crack,' he revealed later. 'After testing at Imola the Thursday after Nürburgring, our physiotherapist had a look and said it was broken. I said well I've been driving with it . . . It wasn't until five days later, when I had it X-rayed in Dublin, that it

was confirmed there was a crack. It was uncomfortable when I was driving in Imola, but it's okay now.'

In Germany he expanded further on his feelings about discipline on the race track. Some of his rivals took his comments with a pinch of salt, bearing in mind his recent incidents, but they had been the result of errors of judgement rather than deliberate, provocative actions, and he saw nothing incongruous in them. 'My concern was simply that from one week to the next there didn't seem to be a clear ruling on what action should be taken. Sometimes action was taken and other times not. That is no good for a driver who needs to know how to approach the matter at each race. Now it appears to have been clarified by the FIA, which has ruled that no holds are barred – as long as our actions are not dangerous. It seems that in terms of overtaking, the regulations have not changed and I can make a protest if I wish. But that's not what we want. The important thing is to have exciting racing, which is what we had in Germany. It is good for the sport, but only so long as it is safe. Or at least as safe as motor racing can be . . .'

Two races followed a week apart in Japan, and in both, Schumacher and Benetton were so crushingly superior that Hill and Williams

In the gravel yet again, here at Monza, Hill finds himself on the end of an aggressive lecture from an angry Michael Schumacher after colliding with the champion for the second time in four races.

crept away. Coulthard and Hill were beaten into second and third places respectively in the Pacific GP at Aida, where Schumacher clinched his second consecutive title, while both crashed out of the Japanese GP at Suzuka. In the latter race, the rancour at Williams reached fever pitch, coinciding for Hill with another bruising from the tabloid press. Key personnel within the team were wondering aloud if they could motivate themselves for another year of such depressing performances, and it is thought that Suzuka was where Frank Williams first initiated the talks with Heinz-Harald Frentzen that led to the option Williams would take up for 1997. 'Things were so bad there,' Hill admitted later, 'that I literally didn't know whether to laugh or to cry. We had sunk so low.'

He tried hard to analyse a situation that was clearly confusing, for so many times in 1995 an apparent upper hand had disappeared mid-race, leaving Hill and Williams in distant second places. It was not just the driver; Williams had produced another great car, but at times, its team management and race strategy was clearly no match for Benetton's.

'It's the real world of Formula One,' Hill said, like a man trying to convince himself of something alien to his innate beliefs. 'A lot of factors have come to bear that I haven't encountered before, because last season was not a typical season at all. This season was a fight for the championship from the very beginning.'

After the FIA had 'clarified' the overtaking rule he had driven with greater aggression, but he admitted that cut and thrust did not really suit his style and manner. 'I don't think it's the picture of sport performed at its highest level that I think Formula One should be. I have my own view about it, but that's just my opinion of it. The fact is that Formula One will be performed in a certain way and I have to get on with what will be accepted practice. I can't change it to suit me. I'm going to have to get on with it as it is.'

Some believed he was a driver who needed a target before he could rise to the occasion, rather than a Senna or a Schumacher who would be quite happy setting up the target for others. 'I don't think so,' he disagreed. 'I make goals for myself. When I started, my goal was always the next level up. This season I made my target winning the World Championship and it's been doubly difficult. Starting from the first race, that slope got steeper!' A rueful laugh accompanied that remark.

Just before the previous year's British Grand Prix he had said: 'When you have a mortgage and children the, World Championship doesn't seem so important,' and now he was criticised for it by those who mistook it for lack of commitment rather than simply a balanced comment from a family man who could see a wider picture. Of all the top drivers he probably has the most stable family life, but when asked how much he draws emotionally on it, his brows would knit as if he had been expecting a rather more awkward question.

'THINGS WERE SO BAD THERE, THAT I LITERALLY DIDN'T KNOW WHETHER TO LAUGH OR TO CRY. WE HAD SUNK SO LOW.'

'It's difficult. I'm not at home much, so it's quite tricky. This year there has been quite a lot of pressure from all sides, because we moved to a different country (Dublin), had a new baby girl; these are all considerations when you have to get the best out of yourself and prepare for Formula One. It becomes less to do with what you are actually doing and more to do with your state of mind. It comes back to not being pressured into doing things that you don't really believe are right.'

Switching off from racing was a problem, he admitted, but not necessarily something he really wanted to do for long. 'You can't separate things. If I am given enough time at home I can switch off . . .' He laughed. 'But it doesn't take long before I am thinking about the next race! The wonderful thing about being a Grand Prix driver is that you are presented sixteen times in a season with a challenge that you can focus on, and it's something that's never more than a fortnight away. It's a tangible goal each time, and it's very appealing to live like that. The trouble is your life goes up and down each time!'

He had a simple aim as he bounced back for 1996, just as Nigel Mansell did in 1986 and '87. 'My goal is to perform better than I have performed recently, and to try and win races. I'm a better driver now than I was last year.'

1995 had been a crucible, forging a stronger driver. Hill laughed at the thought, his face darkening as the bushy eyebrows knitted again. 'What, you mean like sort of being glazed? It is like steel being tempered, and you feel like you've been hit with a hammer! I've certainly been hammered a few times!'

Hill and Coulthard had got on reasonably well as team-mates, but for 1996 the Scot was switching to McLaren as Williams plumped for Jacques Villeneuve, the highly rated Canadian who was the son of legendary Ferrari star Gilles Villeneuve, who died in qualifying for the Belgian GP in 1982. But be-

fore the change around there was one final race, the Australian GP at Adelaide. It was the last race in the state before Victoria and Melbourne were scheduled to take over, and there was the usual end-of-term atmosphere. Damon and Georgie had escaped to Bali after the desperation of Suzuka. They were on their own, without the children for the first time virtually since Oliver had been born, and they savoured their time together in the Four Seasons Hotel. Hill arrived in Australia a new man, so much so that Frank Williams noticed it almost immediately. 'It was quite extraordinary,' he revealed. 'I asked him what he had done to himself, and he just laughed and said he'd gone away and had a long think about things, and got his head together.'

And indeed he had. The Australian GP yielded him a crushing victory, but ironically the seeds of Hill's rejection by Williams the following August had already been sown. New man or not, it would transpire that he was now racing for the team on borrowed time.

Back on top: in Adelaide, Hill emerged a new man after taking the time to rebuild himself psychologically in the wake of his disastrous Japanese tour. The result was a crushing victory, ironically enough his thirteenth.

7

CHAMPION OF THE WORLD

EVERY NEW GRAND PRIX SEASON APPEARS TO HOLD THE
PROMISE OF BEING THE MOST OPEN AND COMPETITIVE
FOR YEARS, AND 1996 SEEMED NO EXCEPTION.
SCHUMACHER HAD SWITCHED TO FERRARI, IN EXCHANGE
FOR JEAN ALESI AND GERHARD BERGER WHO WENT TO
BENETTON. THIS PLACED DAMON HILL FIRMLY ON POLE
POSITION TO WIN THE WORLD CHAMPIONSHIP, AND EVEN
BEFORE THE SHOCK NEWS MID-SEASON, IT WAS FELT
IT WOULD BE NOW OR NEVER.

In 1995 Hill had looked a potential champion for the first three races until Benetton gave Schumacher an improved car, and from then on his challenge fell apart. After the promise of 1993 and 1994, 1995 was easily his worst full season in F1, but he learned an immense amount from it. Like Nigel Mansell, he bounced back from it a stronger driver and a more rounded individual. If you took away the psychological pressures that he had in 1995, many of which Williams created and which led to a lot of his mistakes, he had proved himself at least as good as anybody bar Schumacher, and being perhaps a half second a lap slower than the double World Champion was certainly no disgrace. He also had the experience to put together a full championship campaign. He had paid his dues in full.

Villeneuve's speed surprised many, but not Hill, when the season opened at the new Albert Park track in Melbourne. On a circuit which nobody knew, and on which his lack of F1 experience was thus less of a disadvantage, Villeneuve took a sensational pole position and led by inches from Hill, until the pressure from behind forced him into an error at the first corner. Jacques survived that, but as

the onboard telemetry warned that he had damaged an oil pipe, he was advised to back off in order to make the finish. Hill sped home the winner after an intelligent run in which he had not threatened to jeopardise sixteen valuable points for Williams with any rash overtaking moves, and equalled his father's score of fourteen GP triumphs.

He repeated the successes in Brazil and Argentina, before recovering from a disastrous start in the European GP at the Nürburgring, to take fourth place. Villeneuve won for the first time there, beating Schumacher's surprisingly reliable new Ferrari V10, but when Hill bounced back to beat Schumacher in the San Marino GP at Imola, the status quo was restored. At this stage nobody else had the combination of speed, reliability and racecraft to offer a serious challenge. Schumacher's car was obviously not fully competitive, McLaren-Mercedes were struggling yet again even though Coulthard had led briefly at Imola, Alesi and Berger had been rudely surprised by the wayward behaviour of Benetton's new challenger. Even Villeneuve had lost a little momentum as he was learning new tracks the hard way.

The first chinks in the armour appeared at Monaco and Barcelona. In the principality

Well done, old chap! Hill won the opening race of 1996, in Melbourne, but was first to congratulate new team-mate Jacques Villeneuve on a stunning début.

that his father had made his own personal race track, Hill had this time lost out to Schumacher in the battle for pole position, and a great race was expected on a wet track. But far from Schumacher leaping into the lead and then resolutely defending it on a circuit on which overtaking is well nigh impossible, it was Hill who took the initiative at the start. And further sensation came when Schumacher crashed halfway round the lap, sliding terminally into a kerb on the right-hand corner just after the Loews hairpin. Until the forty-first lap Hill was in complete control, striding majestically towards the family's sixth podium appointment with the Grimaldi family, but then came a puff of smoke as he went into the tunnel, and on the run down the seafront towards the chicane he pulled off. A nut had loosened on his Renault V10's oil pump.

The Spanish GP was a different kind of disaster, as Schumacher ran away and hid in very wet conditions and it was Hill's turn to crash ignominiously. He had opted not to adjust his car's ride height, and it aquaplaned out of control. 'The car was far too nervous,' he said, 'but I couldn't try driving it slowly because you need the speed to generate the downforce . . .'

He won again in Canada and France, beating Villeneuve both times, and took pole position for the British GP, but Villeneuve won there after Hill made a bad start and spun into retirement when a front wheel loosened.

Hill won again in Germany, when Gerhard Berger's engine exploded with three laps left, but he had again made a poor start and this was becoming cause for concern. Villeneuve liked the two-pedal system of throttle and brake, with a hand clutch, but Hill preferred the standard system with a foot clutch as well. 'The problem for Damon,' Patrick Head explained succinctly, 'is that he's got three pedals and only two feet. And if he's got one foot on the accelerator and one foot on the clutch, he hasn't got one for the brake to stop the car edging forward.'

Villeneuve won in Hungary after another poor start from Hill, while Schumacher took

the Belgian GP from Villeneuve with Hill only fifth, well down in the spare car after damaging his engine in a spin in his race car during the morning warm-up.

Since the German GP at Hockenheim, speculation had raged that Williams was going to replace Hill with Heinz-Harald Frentzen for 1997. This was strongly denied by all concerned, but after Spa it emerged that Frank Williams had indeed terminated negotiations. It was a massive blow, at a crucial part of the championship fight.

For the second year in succession, Hill dominated the Brazilian GP, but this time he was still in front by the chequered flag.

The previous year, when relations were more tense, Hill had outlined just what driving for Williams meant to him. 'I'm very happy here, but to some degree, in the back of your mind, you wonder what it might be like somewhere else at times. I've been here for five years, and there's no point in changing just for the sake of it. But there's the possibility of being regarded as part of the furniture. I've grown within the company, which sometimes presents its own problems. But I want to give myself the best opportunity to win, and that's what Williams gives me.'

And if he had to move? 'Any one of the top four teams. Ferrari would be an exciting idea; there are many, many problems associated with driving for Ferrari and it demands a lot from the driver. Then there's the pressure from the Italian media, but I wouldn't understand what they were saying!' He had laughed then, but when the crunch finally came, it was no laughing matter.

At the end of 1995, when Coulthard had been obliged to switch to McLaren, Hill had given a completely candid response when asked whether he felt sorry for the Scot. 'If you want the honest answer, no. This is a hard game, and the same rules apply to him as much as to myself. This is a fickle business. . .' To his great credit, he now refused to feel sorry for himself, no matter how crushing a blow he had been dealt.

In retrospect, the first half of his season re-flected the high level of his confidence, but the second half was nowhere near so cohesive. Close observers kept coming back to the same thing. How much psychological impact did Frank's decision really have?

Hill could afford to laugh a little later on as he savoured his title and pondered the question. 'Well,' he said with a smile, 'it wasn't quite the pat on the back I'd been expecting! I've got used to it now. Every season there is some kind of drama that crops up to try and put you off balance, but I really had the rug pulled out from under me there.

'The only thing I wanted from this season was to win the championship. What was going to happen after the last race was something I'd almost dismissed as irrelevant. I'd never even looked beyond the end of the season to begin with. I started out simply with the intention of winning the title this time. Whilst it was a bit of a blow, finding out that I wouldn't be driving for the team while I was still leading the World Championship, I was determined that I'd rather come away with something than come away without the drive and without the championship either.'

Despite the acute disappointment, and whatever personal feelings he still harbours – he rather pointedly thanked neither Williams nor Patrick Head upon winning the title – he was objective enough to assess the role they had played in his success. 'There has to be given a lot of credit to the way Frank and

To the victor, the spoils. And a congratulatory hug from wife Georgie. This was Argentina.

Patrick run the team, and also to all members of the team. They are very, very fair and I never, ever had any kind of uneven treatment. They are meticulous about that. They always give each guy the best chance that they can give him of winning races.'

Opinion remains divided why Williams dropped him. Some suggest that his feeble performance at Spa was the final straw, that Frank was concerned that such a showing was not going to win races in 1997 against Schumacher in a fully competitive Ferrari. Insiders hinted that Williams did not care to be dictated to by Hill's manager, Michael Breen. One even went so far as to suggest: 'If Damon had done his own negotiating, he'd still be driving for us.'

Whatever, there was a championship to be clinched, and at Monza for the Italian GP Damon responded in the best possible way by taking pole position. And this time he made a good start, though not as good as Alesi, who went into the lead like a rocket in the Benetton. But Hill was in very determined form, and grabbed the lead from the Frenchman in the second Lesmo corner. Jean hung on and they went side-by-side into Ascari, but Damon resolutely held his line and Alesi was obliged to back off. Hill seemed to have it made as he eased open a two-second lead by the end of the fifth lap, but then came disaster. Going into the first chicane, he inexplicably hit one of the tyre barriers that he and Schumacher had requested after an incident in practice when another driver had cut across the kerbs and thrown up a large chunk of concrete at Villeneuve. The Williams spun and came to rest under an advertising bridge, and an agonised Hill sat with his helmeted head in his hands. He had thrown away not just the race but, quite possibly it seemed at that moment, the championship. And all through an unforced error of cataclysmic proportions.

Later, he could joke about it. 'I didn't touch the tyres, I clouted them! It would have been nice to have won in Monza, but I think that things sort of pan out for some strange cosmic reason. I mean, there we were in Italy

and Michael won. Although it wasn't me in the Ferrari, it was quite a special event and it added to the tension over the rest of the season. I wouldn't have it any other way, the way the championship turned out. But I am pretty cheesed off that I hit the tyres!' It was a typical Hill expression, 'cheesed off'. But he was less cheesed off than he might have been, for on a day when the gods were looking out for him, both Villeneuve and Frentzen also made similar errors.

It seemed the aggression which took him back past Alesi on the opening lap might well have been the quality which cost him the race, as if he had difficulty balancing it with neces-

After his defeat by Hill in Canada, Villeneuve was hungry to turn the tables at Silverstone, where he and Hill enjoyed a moment of humour with legendary commentator, Murray Walker.

sary prudence, but his explanation was revealing. 'The things that go through your mind when you're in the lead of a race are those things which determine your mode of driving. I made a very aggressive start. Thereafter I was determined to drive more cautiously. But sometimes in the attempt to drive more cautiously you can make mistakes. I won't be the first or the last driver to make a mistake in those circumstances. I would love to have a perfect C.V., but show me a driver who has.'

The Portuguese GP at Estoril gave him another chance to put the title away, and before the race he played down the growing pressure on himself and Villeneuve, who was still only thirteen points behind and was beginning to look like a man on a roll. 'I don't think there's a build-up of pressure here. I feel quite relaxed, not anxious. My nerves are not jangling, as some people who would have you believe. I'm looking forward to this weekend. Jacques and I have got a good relationship. We both want to win and there are no problems between us.'

A newspaper had tried to play up the situation, alleging that Villeneuve was unhappy that Hill had squeezed him too hard at the start of some races, but Hill's response was straightforward. 'Jacques is at liberty to do what he likes. It's been tough all season. From Melbourne he made it plain from the start that he was not prepared to be pushed around. Nothing's changed. I'm not surprised the championship has come down to the line. I've always said you can't predict what's going to happen, that because you've got a twenty-point lead mid-season or have won three races on the trot, it's going to be a walkover. It's very rarely been like that.'

Again he took pole position, and after a

Germany brought Hill one of his luckier victories, when Gerhard Berger's Benetton blew its engine with three laps to go, but it was just recompense for the disappointment of Monte Carlo.

perience to the full. And as Damon got himself flummoxed in traffic and Jacques got into his stride, the lead changed hands in the final pit stops. Hill admitted that the better driver had won on the day, and afterwards looked shellshocked as he tried to figure out where that initial advantage had gone. It didn't help when former champion Niki Lauda, whose example in borrowing money to reach the top Hill had followed ten years earlier, said: 'I've never seen anyone go to so much trouble to lose the World Championship.' Yet that was how it looked. Villeneuve was the man in form, and Hill seemed to be tottering, outpsyched by that mid-season upset. As they prepared for the final race in Japan, their showdown distilled to this: Villeneuve was nine points behind and had to win the race, with Hill placed lower than sixth. If Hill was sixth they would each have eighty-eight points, but Hill would win the title because of seven wins to Villeneuve's five.

Before that, however, Damon had a surprise

great start he had built a sixteen-second lead as Villeneuve lay trapped in fourth place behind Alesi and Schumacher. But then the Canadian pulled a startling move on the World Champion by slipping by on the outside of the final corner, using his IndyCar experience to spring on the world, and it came on 27 September when he announced that he would be driving for Tom Walkinshaw's TWR Arrows team in 1997. Seasoned observers had expected a deal with Jordan-Peugeot, or possibly even Jackie Stewart's new team, when

plans to ease Alesi out of Benetton and slide Hill into his place came to nothing after Monza. But this caught everyone unprepared, especially Eddie Jordan himself. Walkinshaw, a no-nonsense Scot, had invited Hill to his technical base at Leafield, and there Hill had been amazed to see facilities the equal of Williams. The deal had been done that day.

'I took on board all the factors that were in front of me when I was considering which way to go,' Hill said. 'I won't say the exact reasons why I preferred to go with TWR over the others, all of which had their own merits. It wasn't an easy decision to make, but the truth of the matter is that I opted for Tom Walkinshaw and TWR Arrows for a number of reasons and I think that on balance that was going to be the best combination for me.'

Walkinshaw is a racer, and he could see the benefit of having the best test driver in the business in one of his cars, whether he won the championship or not. That support was a key element as Hill moved forward to the most crucial race of his career, amid all the foolish suggestions that he could clinch the title by the simple expedient of pushing Villeneuve off the track. It would not be the first time such tactics had been seen at Suzuka, but Hill treated the suggestions with

the disdain they deserved.

'If I am in the lead, I will defend my position vigorously. There is no question about it,' he said. 'But I don't want to resort to unfair tactics. It's always a matter of opinion what is fair and what is not. I drive the way I feel fits at any given time, and I'm at liberty to drive in a way which may not be the way that people expect me to drive. I don't always have to give way. What I am saying is that I'm currently leading the championship and I am determined to win it. But I am against unfair tactics; I have seen championships settled in the past in ways that I regard as unsatisfactory, and I don't want it to happen this time.

'Clearly, I feel I can win the championship on merit, on driver performance. There are all sorts of views about how drivers should conduct themselves on the circuit, and some drivers have differing views to my own. I don't have any ambition to be involved in that kind of tactic. I don't agree with driving into the back of someone at the start of the race, just to make sure that they don't have the chance of winning the championship. I didn't agree with it at half past three in the morning when I got up to watch the Japanese Grand Prix on television in 1990 and Senna did it to Prost. I was really irritated. We missed a good race.

On top of the world, the reality of his achievement finally begins to sink in as a champagne-drenched Hill stands atop the podium in Suzuka.

'Alternatively, when Alain was racing there at Suzuka the previous year, he did what he was entitled to do, which was to turn into the corner. It wasn't as if Ayrton had not pushed him to the very limit of what he could endure, with that particular brand of intimidation that he used. At that point what Alain did was perfectly within the rules.' Those words would have an interesting ring to them.

Villeneuve took pole position with Hill alongside after a late effort moved him to the front row for the sixteenth time in the season, but the Canadian seemed to handle the pressure better, and Hill looked edgy. But when it really mattered it was Villeneuve who screwed up his start, as Hill surged into a lead he never lost. Following a nasty little display at the post-qualifying conference, when Villeneuve and Schumacher had deliberately kept talking to one another when it was Hill's turn to answer questions, it was a satisfying way in which to have the last laugh.

'I won't make it sound more difficult than it was, but Suzuka is quite tricky,' Hill ex-

plained. 'The track slopes down so if you actually take your foot off the brake and the car rolls forward you get a penalty.' This should have favoured Villeneuve, with his two-pedal system and manual clutch. 'That required a little bit of trick technique because I don't left-foot brake like Jacques does. So I was worried about that and I thought Jacques was going to have the advantage there over me, but everything went well and I got a good start. I'd said before that if I got into the lead, I wanted to stay there. I knew that the right approach to the race was to use attack as the best form of defence.'

His sole moment of alarm came in the chicane on the third lap, when Gerhard Berger tried to do to him what Senna had done to Prost there in that 1989 event. 'I saw him in my mirrors and just carried on doing what I always do. Next thing I knew, he was way back. Once he'd decided to go for it there wasn't much I could do. It wasn't as if I could accelerate. I'd just got to the chicane. I just carried on doing what I was doing, and left him to

Man and wife, father and mother, champion and first lady: Damon and Georgie Hill bring a rare dignity and sense of family values to the world of Formula One.

make his own arrangements.' It looked very close ... 'It did, didn't it?' Hill enquired disingenuously, to uproarious laughter.

Damon Hill, they had said, lacked bottle, lacked the aggression for close combat. But in the previous two races Jean Alesi had learned a lesson, and now so had Gerhard Berger.

When Villeneuve, pushing hard but still down in fourth place, lost a wheel on his thirty-seventh lap, Hill became champion of the world. Yet it was not an easy moment when he learned of his team-mate's demise. 'When they told me, I went into a bit of a spin in my head for a few laps, because I came to the realisation that I didn't actually have to carry on driving any more!' he revealed.

'It was strange, really. When he dropped out it was all done and there were still fifteen laps to go. But I thought, "What the hell, I might as well carry on. I've come this far ..." And it was well worth pushing on to the end. To have won the race, my last drive for Williams, and to have won the championship all in one event, was just more than I ever expected.'

Amid emotional scenes he embraced Georgie, and paid lengthy tribute to those who had helped him to climb the mountain. 'I feel like I'm on a rocket that's just taken off,' he admitted. 'It's just a wonderful relief of pressure and sense of satisfaction.' And when the champagne had been washed out of his hair and they had flown home to England three days later, the whirlwind continued.

'I'm absolutely overwhelmed with the reception that I've had, from the moment I stepped off the plane at Heathrow, I've been mobbed,' Hill laughed. 'I haven't had much sleep since I got out of the car – I didn't get much before I got into it, actually! Right now I don't feel tired, just elated. I'm supercharged. I got up at four this morning!'

In the end it had become the fairy tale, a perfect end, despite the worrying moments. He laughed again. 'Were you worried? No! It was always going to turn out well. I think things happen for the right reasons, and the finish was so exciting. In Adelaide in '94 it came down to the last race and was all the more thrilling for it. Formula One really has put on a fantastic show for the last few years, and I've been very privileged to be able to run at the front and enjoy race wins and the attention. It's a tremendously rewarding feeling.'

And now that his name was in the record books forever – Damon Hill, World Champion 1996 – he answered the critics who had suggested he would never make it. 'There are always going to be critics, and there have been of everyone who's ever raced. It's really just a matter of looking at somebody's results and saying, given these circumstances how much better could you expect somebody to do? I won half the races this season, and I've still won more races than any of my team-mates, apart from Alain Prost, which was a slightly different situation. I believe I couldn't be asked to do any more. I'm very happy with what I did. I've never claimed to be perfect.

'There was a story I read about Jack Nicklaus, who was reading something that had been written about him saying that he was washed up, finished. So he cut it out and stuck it on his fridge door, and went out and won his fifth Masters, or whatever it was. It's possible to use it to motivate yourself, and prove people wrong, but that's not the only factor. It's part of the business.

'From now on it's going to be a little easier to enjoy things. As I said, it's in the record books, it's down there forever. It can't be taken away. I achieved what I set out to achieve. I'm fully satisfied.'

Georgie paid her own moving tribute. 'All the people who thought Damon couldn't do it, that he wasn't good enough to do it, can now see that he has actually done it. All the setbacks he's had, he's overcome, and he's proved himself to have more integrity and dignity in his little finger than most people have got in their whole body. I'm just thrilled for him and really proud of him.'

Frank Williams looked pleased, though as ever it was hard to tell his true thoughts. 'Obviously I have mixed feelings for Jacques, but overall we can look back over a great season. In many ways it's more appropriate for Damon to win, because he's worked hard for four years. He's climbed the mountain, and he's now at the top. He deserves to be there.'

Patrick Head, who had always had a soft spot for Hill, said: 'It's absolutely brilliant.

He's won eight Grands Prix, and to win a World Championship by winning a race straight from the front like that . . . He had it well in control. We could see from the telemetry that he was driving very conservatively, well within his limits.'

Hill had contributed 69 of the 168 points Williams accrued while winning its sixth Constructors' Championship in 1993, 91 of 118 with its seventh in 1994, and 97 of the remarkable 175 it scored with its record-equalling eighth in 1996, not to mention 69 of its 112 as runner-up to Benetton in 1995. He played a role in four Constructors' titles, and scored twenty-one wins, twenty pole positions and nineteen fastest laps.

More than that, he helped to pull the team through the darkness after Senna's accident. 'Whatever Damon's problems were – and it was obviously a very difficult time for us – he handled himself very well under very difficult circumstances and was very supportive to the guys in the team,' said Head. 'You know, one of the nicest things about Damon is that he is normal, and I don't mean that in a derogatory manner. He's just a normal bloke, a family man. It was just nice to work with a driver who didn't treat all of the talented people who work at Williams as if they were just minions there to do his bidding.'

Proud, too, was William Taylor, a seventeen-year-old from Brackley, near Silverstone, who had been a devoted fan since watching him in the 1993 British GP. He had never missed one of Hill's test sessions at his local track, and had even gone to Portugal, courtesy of Williams. But when his telephone rang on the Thursday afternoon before the Japanese GP, he had suspected a hoax when Brigitte Hill asked: 'Damon is wondering whether you'd like to go to Japan to see him race.'

'Damon asked me in Portugal if I was going to Japan and I joked and said I would be if I won the lottery,' Taylor explained. 'He said, "Oh, I was looking forward to your support there!" Then obviously he arranged it all for me afterwards.'

In the euphoric aftermath, Taylor dined with the Hills and was part of their impromptu karaoke session in Suzuka's infamous Log Cabin, where once an inebriated Ayrton Senna had celebrated his own first world title. Teetotal, non-smoking Hill had already had schnapps and a cigar pressed upon him by Rothmans' motorhome manager Karl-Heinz Zimmermann, and was feeling mellow.

Taylor still can't quite believe that he really did go to Japan. 'You read about Damon being gloomy and grumpy, but being out with him just proves what a really nice guy he is. A great sense of humour and personality. For him to do something like this for me … it's just brilliant.'

While other public figures ensure that their good works are conveniently recorded by strategically placed observers, Hill said nothing to anyone about his invitation. It was not a publicity stunt, but the selfless act of a thoughtful man, in whom the sport saw a perfect ambassador.

Thus Damon Hill finally emulated his father Graham, to become the first World

Champion son of a World Champion. 'I've read a lot about trying to live up to a father's record and all that,' he said calmly, 'and it's nonsense. My father died twenty-one years ago, and that's an awfully long time. I've long since handled that emotion. The season this year was something that I wanted to do. I'd got myself into the situation and had set out in the past intent on winning the championship. And I was doing it for me and for all the reasons that were relevant in 1996, not rooted in the past.'

'The great thing about Formula One is that it attracts the best drivers. It is the pinnacle. It means so much more to race against the very best, and I regard myself as one of the very best. That's where you really push the limits, where you really find out what it's like to drive on the edge, and that's what all drivers are after. It is the ultimate test.'

In 1996 it was an ultimate test that a dignified sportsman passed with flying colours.

The end of the line: with the final chequered flag of 1996, the curtain came down on Hill's career with the Williams team. Having earlier bid an emotional farewell to the mechanics on Villeneuve's car, the new champion said goodbye to the men who had been so instrumental in helping him to achieve the great goal.

First published in Great Britain in 1994
entitled *Damon Hill: Legacy of Speed* by
George Weidenfeld and Nicolson Ltd
The Orion Publishing Group
Orion House
5 Upper St Martin's Lane
London WC2H 9EA

This revised edition published in
Great Britain in 1996.

A catalogue record for this book is available
from the British Library.

ISBN 0 297 82262 4

Designed by Bradbury & Williams Ltd, London.
Litho origination by Pixel Colour Ltd, London.
Printed and bound by Butler & Tanner Ltd,
Frome and London.

Picture Credits
All photographs are © John Townsend except:
Endpapers Graham Hill with four-year-old Damon
(Popperfoto).